Most Valuable Baseball Cards

Christopher Benjamin

A Perigee Book

Perigee Books
are published by
The Putnam Publishing Group
200 Madison Avenue
New York, NY 10016

An MBKA Production
Suite 27F, 1725 York Avenue
New York, NY 10128

ACKNOWLEDGMENTS
Thanks are due to the following for providing the cards illustrated:
The Card Collector's Archive, Larry Fortuck, Peter Gilleeny,
Alan (Mr. Mint) Rosen, Tony Salamone, and Joshua Evans of Lelands.
Card values were obtained from Beckett Publications
and from the Hobby Card Index.
All card prices listed apply to "excellent" specimens
unless otherwise noted in the text.

Library of Congress Cataloging-in-Publication Data

Benjamin, Christopher.
    Most valuable baseball cards / Chris Benjamin.
        p.   cm.
    ISBN 0-399-51592-5 : $10.95
    1. Baseball cards—United States—History.   I. Title.
GV875.3.B46   1990   89-38799   CIP
769'.49796357'0973—dc20

Printed in Hong Kong
1 2 3 4 5 6 7 8 9 10

Introduction

What history considers brilliant invention is often more a result of circumstance than of individual genius. So it was with the trading card. The post-Civil War period in America was a time of great change. Our society was in the process of being reshaped by the forces of the Industrial Revolution and the new technologies which accompanied it. The urbanization so necessary for economic development demanded new business methods such as mass-marketing, national advertising, improved product packaging, and large-scale distribution networks. In this fiercely competitive marketplace, any new strategy to improve sales was welcome.

To our knowledge, the earliest trading card was issued with "Marquis of Lorne" cigarettes in 1879. What made this card unique? Simply that it was placed *inside* the package with the cigarettes, rather than handed directly to the customer over the counter like the thousands of advertising cards before it. This simple idea — putting a collectible advertising card inside the package — launched the trading-card era.

For the first thirty years, trading cards were almost exclusively issued with tobacco products. About 1910, the candy companies entered the card game; they, in turn, were supplanted by the great bubble gum manufacturers of the 1930s, 1940s and 1950s. Today most collectors associate trading-cards with bubble gum, although cards have been issued with a multitude of products over the years. Baseball has been the most popular subject of trading cards since the earliest times and the cards pictured in this book are the most valuable not only in terms of price, but in scarcity and popularity as well.

One of the earliest card sets ever produced in America, Goodwin Tobacco's 1887–1890 photographic series, is simply amazing in terms of length and variety. It contains over 6,000 different photos of baseball players, pugilists, stage personalities, and world celebrities.

The cards are actual sepia-tone photos glued onto cardboard, and the most valuable pictures are those depicting Hall of Famers like Anson ($900) and Ward ($350), or special "Brown's Champions 1886" like Latham ($175).

R. L. CARUTHERS.
ALLEN & GINTER'S
RICHMOND. *Cigarettes* VIRGINIA.

To compete with Goodwin's popular photographic cards (p. 3), tobacco rival Allen & Ginter issued a two-part series entitled "World's Champions" in 1887–88. Created with superb color artwork, it is the most popular of all the nineteenth-century baseball sets. The first series contains ten baseball players with a total market value of $4300.

JOSEPH MULVEY.
ALLEN & GINTER'S
RICHMOND. *Cigarettes* VIRGINIA.

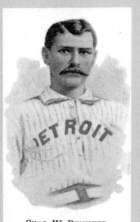

CHAS. W. BENNETT.
ALLEN & GINTER'S
RICHMOND. *Cigarettes* VIRGINIA.

CHARLES COMISKEY.
ALLEN & GINTER'S
RICHMOND. *Cigarettes* VIRGINIA.

CAPT. JACK GLASSCOCK.
ALLEN & GINTER'S
RICHMOND. *Cigarettes* VIRGINIA.

JOHN CLARKSON.
ALLEN & GINTER'S
RICHMOND. *Cigarettes* VIRGINIA.

JOHN M. WARD.
ALLEN & GINTER'S
RICHMOND. *Cigarettes* VIRGINIA.

TIMOTHY KEEFE.
ALLEN & GINTER'S
RICHMOND. *Cigarettes* VIRGINIA.

MIKE KELLY.
ALLEN & GINTER'S
RICHMOND. *Cigarettes* VIRGINIA.

ADRIAN C. ANSON.
ALLEN & GINTER'S
RICHMOND. *Cigarettes* VIRGINIA.

In 1888, Allen & Ginter needed a gimmick to promote sales of a new and larger package of Richmond Straight Cut cigarettes. The result: a "giant" version of their "World's Champions, Second Series," created by adding "backgrounds" to the basic designs. Although the small and large varieties were issued concurrently, collectors agree that the large-size card is harder to find. Of the six cards produced, Ewing's is valued at $1250; the other five are worth $1000 each.

1/2 Detroit and St. Louis, pennant winners of the National League and American Association, met in a slam-bang championship series after the 1887 regular season. To commemorate this famous showdown, an unidentified manufacturer created eighteen die-cut pictures of Detroit and St. Louis players for use as scrapbook paste-ins. Rarely found undamaged, baseball "Scraps" such as Comiskey ($300) and Hanlon ($200) are rare mementos of a classic matchup of baseball titans.

3/4 The stilted mannerisms and static play that characterized nineteenth-century baseball have been preserved for collectors in this pic-turesque series issued by Buchner Tobacco in 1887. The basic flaws of the set, standardization of individual features and duplication of designs, have kept prices relatively low. The two cards pictured here depict Hall of Fame pitcher "Hoss" Radbourn, a 60-game winner in 1884. They sell for $175 apiece.

5 The "Champions of Games and Sports" series was distributed in Kimball cigarettes in 1888. Of the fifty cards in this scarce set, only four portray baseball players. This card of Dell Darling, a Chicago utility player with more personality than talent, carries a hefty $500 price tag.

ANSON, (1st Base, CHICAGO.)

BROUTHERS, (1st Base, DETROIT.)

Goodwin, already enjoying a huge market success with its photographic cards, nevertheless recognized the threat posed by the color lithographs issued by rival tobacco companies. In 1888, the firm produced a fifty-card "Champions" set, in color, to compete directly with similar sets from Allen & Ginter and Kimball. Eight ballplayers, seven from the National League and one from the American Association, represent baseball in the "Champions" set (total value: $5200).

GLASSCOCK S.S. INDIANAPOLIS

KEEFE, (P. NEW YORK.)

KELLY, (C. BOSTON.)

CARUTHERS, (P. Brooklyn.)

DUNLAP (Capt. Pittsburg.)

Cabinet cards — extra-large pictures of famous athletes, stage personalities, and other interesting celebrities — were actually designed to be displayed in the home. Hence the name.

1/2   In contrast to the standard cabinet card of the times — usually a black-and-white or sepia photograph glued to a cardboard mount — tobacco manufacturer Duke commissioned studio portraits to be hand-colored and then lithographed. These handsome cards, issued in 1893, were probably handed out to customers in tobacco stores. Only four baseball subjects

are known: an untrimmed Delehanty would sell for $2000 and Nash is valued at $1500

3/4   The cards of the 1894 "Newsboy" cabinet series were obtained in exchange for package tags and coupons, and may also have been handed out or sold at newsstands and tobacconists. If the numbering system on the cards is correct, over eight hundred were issued, but only ten baseball subjects are known. Ward and Rusie, New York stars and future Hall of Famers, are currently the most valuable of these, listing at $1000 each.

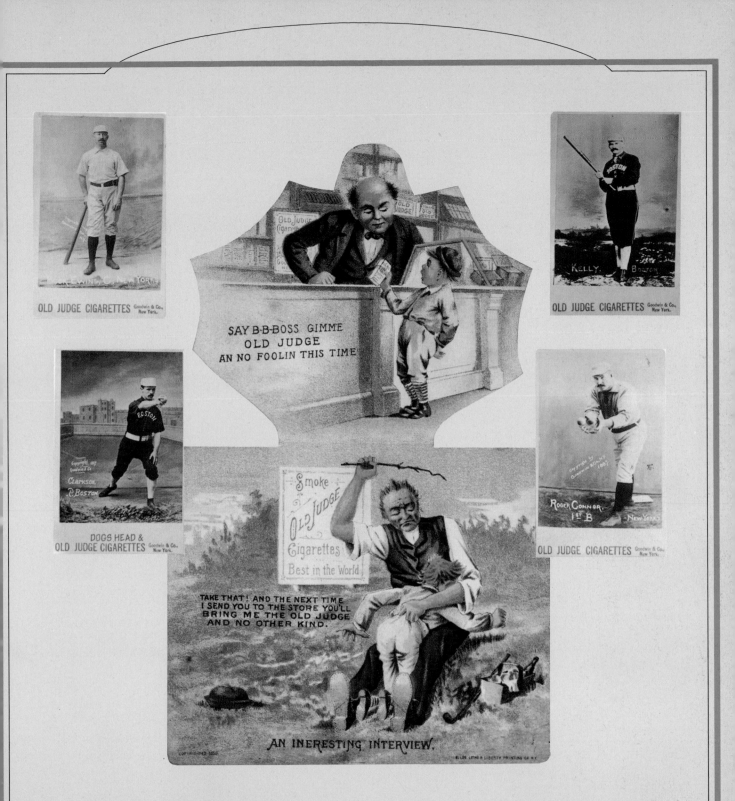

OLD JUDGE CIGARETTES Goodwin & Co., New York.

OLD JUDGE CIGARETTES Goodwin & Co., New York.

SAY B-B-BOSS GIMME OLD JUDGE AN NO FOOLIN THIS TIME.

DOGS HEAD & OLD JUDGE CIGARETTES Goodwin & Co., New York.

ROGER CONNOR, 1st B. New York.

OLD JUDGE CIGARETTES Goodwin & Co., New York.

Smoke OLD JUDGE Cigarettes Best in the World

TAKE THAT! AND THE NEXT TIME I SEND YOU TO THE STORE YOU'LL BRING ME THE OLD JUDGE AND NO OTHER KIND.

AN INERESTING INTERVIEW.

The New York–based Goodwin Company offered more "elegant Cabinet Photographs" of baseball players than any of its competitors. An 1888 advertising card tells us that each cabinet card was exchanged for thirty-five of the proof-of-purchase certificates packed with Old Judge and Gypsy Queen cigarettes. In 1889, the exchange rate was lowered to twenty certificates per card.

Goodwin offered cabinet photographs "of every player of prominence in any club in the country," and the names of several hundred subjects from the National League, Western Association, and American Association appear on an 1889 checklist (see p. 56). Illustrated: Ewing ($500), Kelly ($750), Clarkson ($500), and Connor ($600).

1   THE PRESIDENTIAL B. B. CLUB.

HONEST LONG-CUT CHEWING AND SMOKING

W. DUKE, SONS & CO., N.Y.

2   "Smoke and Chew Little Rhody Cut Plug"

3   A FOUL CATCH.

4   BASE BALL BATTER

1   Grover Cleveland won the popular vote in three presidential elections (1884, 1888 and 1892) but was made President only twice (the electoral college stymied him in 1888). In a possibly derisive tribute to his persistence, the Duke tobacco firm issued this "Presidential B.B. Club" set in 1888, setting Cleveland's oversized head onto bodies taken from a rival's popular "Women Baseball Player" series. These satiric cards are worth $35 per pose . . . but are occasionally offered at much higher prices as genuine baseball cards of an "unknown player"!

2   The tobacco manufacturers of the nineteenth century tried to blend the themes of feminine beauty and baseball whenever possible. In most cases, cards showing women playing baseball are not popular with modern collectors. An exception is this "Base Ball Scene," marketed by George Young. It has a full month of the 1892 National League schedule printed on the back and is valued at $100.

3   The charming "Talk of the Diamond" set was published by Duke in 1893. A scene on one side of the card defines the caption in baseball terms, while another vignette shows its satirical interpretation according to the social mores of the day. A typical card of this set costs $25.

4   The popularity of baseball was evident in Goodwin's 1889 series "Games and Sports." Four cards carry baseball scenes in a set where no other sport has more than one card. The designs incorporate a handsome woman in uniform with a baseball "action" tableau alongside: batter, catcher, fielder, pitcher. Value: $35 each.

A New Century Of Baseball

GOCHNAUER, S.S., Cleveland

One of a hundred and fifty prominent Baseball players

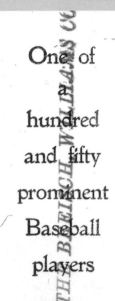

M. CROSS, S.S., Athletic

One of a hundred and fifty prominent Baseball players

Trading cards originated as promotional items designed by rival tobacco companies specifically to sell cigarettes in a fiercely competitive marketplace. The "Battle of the Brands" lasted less than a decade; by 1895, Duke & Sons had eliminated or absorbed every major rival. Duke's new conglomerate, the American Tobacco Company, monopolized the tobacco industry. There no longer existed any reason to produce tobacco cards.

From 1896 to 1908, only a handful of small, independent tobacco firms produced trading-card sets; none of these pictured baseball players. However, a new industry — candy and gum producers — began issuing cards to pack in their goods. The confectionery market was about to blossom into a major source of baseball cards for American collectors.

Duke recognized that burgeoning confection sales would damage his market among "fad" smokers; at the same time, his market share was being challenged by sales of imported "Turkish" tobacco. To strengthen his position, the American Tobacco Company was directed to create dozens of brilliant and imaginative card sets beginning in 1909. The confection trade followed suit. The famine of trading cards disappeared and collectors soon had a cornucopia of sets to choose from.

James Duke and ATC deserve most of the credit for this renaissance. Some historians say it was a by-product of Duke's greed, but the facts tell another story. By 1909, ATC was so powerful and financially secure, both at home and abroad, that neither Turkish tobacco nor domestic candy could threaten its position. In truth, ATC's trading-card sets were a manifestation of James Duke's personal commitment to excellence. No more proof of this is needed than the dramatic decline in trading-card issues after the American Tobacco Company was fragmented by antitrust legislation in 1912. There were bad times ahead for collectors, but Duke created a generation of true card enthusiasts and a legacy of excellence that is recognized to this day.

The Breisch-Williams candy company issued this series of black-and-white photo cards in 1903 and 1904. Considered a "transition" set between the nineteenth and twentieth centuries, it contains cards of old and new generations of baseball heroes. The expression "common card" does not apply to this set: any card sells for a minimum of $65. A back with the company name stamped over the typeset words increases value by twenty-five percent.

1/2 These colorful cards of Honus Wagner ($300) and "Wee Willie" Keeler ($600) are part of a "Base Ball Series" issued by the American Caramel Company from 1909 to 1911. Keeler, the man who "hit 'em where they ain't," is considered to be one of the scarcest cards in the set.

3 While it appears similar to the cards pictured above, this card of "Babe" Adams ($30) actually belongs to a separate 1910 set honoring the Pittsburgh Pirates, world champions in 1909.

4 Trivia question: Who played third base in the Chicago Cubs' famous Tinker-to-Evers-to-Chance infield? Answer: Harry Steinfeldt ($35), who appeared in a special 1910 American Caramel set spotlighting Cub and White Sox players.

1

2

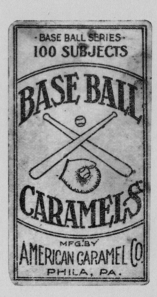

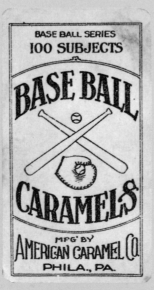

3

4

It was common practice for candy companies to share identical or similar artwork and designs for the fronts of cards. Backs were then "personalized" by specific advertising and layout. The six cards on this page represent five interrelated sets issued during the years 1909 and 1910.

Jennings, Mgr. Detroit Am.

$50

Base Ball Gum.

THIS CARD IS ONE OF A SET OF

50 Base Ball Players

PROMINENT MEMBERS OF NATIONAL AND AMERICAN LEAGUES, ONE OF WHICH IS WRAPPED WITH EVERY PACKAGE OF BASE BALL GUM.

Manufactured only by

JOHN H. DOCKMAN & SONS

Chance, 1b Chicago Nat'l

$50

Play Ball!

AND EAT

Nadja

Caramels

The Winners

Collins, 2b. Phila. Am.

$150

CANDY CROFT'S

CROFT AND ALLEN CO.

Philadelp. Pa.

Lajoie, 2b Cleveland Amer.

$100

CROFT'S SWISS MILK COCOA

Served Hot at Our Fountain 11 South 15th St.

Montague & Co. Philadelphia, Pa.

Cobb, c.f. Detroit Am.

$500

THIS CARD IS ONE OF A SET OF

50 Base Ball Players

PROMINENT MEMBERS OF NATIONAL AND AMERICAN LEAGUES,

Crawford, c.f. Detroit Am.

$75

This Picture is one of a Set of Twenty-five BASE BALL PLAYERS, as follows:

Cobb, Detroit.
Evers, Chicago Nat.
Doyle, New York Nat.
Dooin, Phila. Nat.
Collins, Phila. Am.
Lajoie, Cleveland.
Miller, Pittsburg.
Magee, Phila. Nat.
Tinker, Chicago Nat.
Schmidt, Detroit.
Lobert, Cincinnati.
Wagner, Pittsburg.
Murphy, Phila. Am.
Bender, Phila. Am.
Crawford, Detroit.
Schaefer, Washington.
Matthewson, N. Y. Nat.
Zimmerman, Chicago Nat.
Chase, N. Y. Am.
Bescher, Cincinnati.
Sweak, Boston.
Dougherty, Chicago Am.
Donovan, Detroit.
Kleinow, New York Am.
Knabe, Philadelphia Nat.

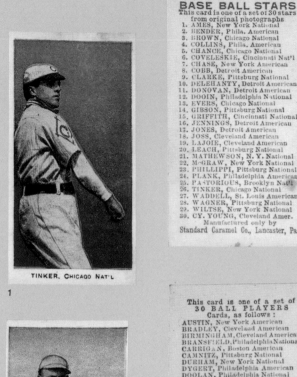

1 This card of Cubs Hall of Fame shortstop Joe Tinker, a 1910 issue from the Standard Caramel Company of Lancaster, Pennsylvania sells for $75.

2 The fact that "Star Base Ball Player" cards were devoid of advertising suggests the publisher sold the designs of this 1911 set to several companies in local markets. The player pictured here, Mickey Doolan ($35), toiled in the big leagues under an assumed name: his real name was Doolittle!

3 C. A. Briggs of Boston distributed the "30 Ball Players" series in 1910. The color card of Cy Young, baseball's winningest pitcher, places him with Boston and is worth $150. The same card with Cleveland as his team ($250) is scarcer.

4/5 The blue-tint card of Young ($75) used the same picture and may have been cut from a candy package. Except for a minor spelling change on one card, all of the Briggs players appeared in a parallel series of black-and-white photos printed on thin, blank-backed paper. They are rarer than the original color set but are not as popular (a typical card costs $40).

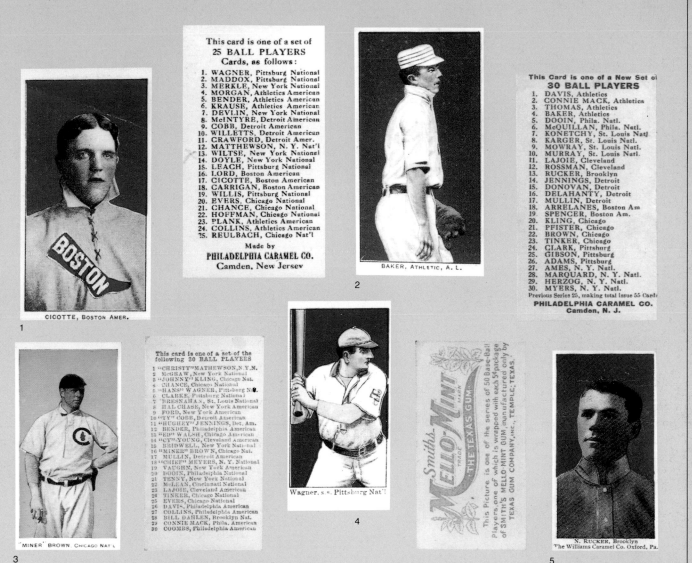

This card is one of a set of
25 BALL PLAYERS
Cards, as follows:

1. WAGNER, Pittsburg National
2. MADDOX, Pittsburg National
3. MERKLE, New York National
4. MORGAN, Athletics American
5. BENDER, Athletics American
6. KRAUSE, Athletics American
7. DEVLIN, New York National
8. McINTYRE, Detroit American
9. COBB, Detroit American
10. WILLETTS, Detroit American
11. CRAWFORD, Detroit Amer.
12. MATTHEWSON, N. Y. Nat'l
13. WILTSE, New York National
14. DOYLE, New York National
15. LEACH, Pittsburg National
16. LORD, Boston American
17. CICOTTE, Boston American
18. CARRIGAN, Boston American
19. WILLIS, Pittsburg National
20. EVERS, Chicago National
21. CHANCE, Chicago National
22. HOFFMAN, Chicago National
23. PLANK, Athletics American
24. COLLINS, Athletics American
25. REULBACH, Chicago Nat'l

Made by
PHILADELPHIA CARAMEL CO.
Camden, New Jersey

CICOTTE, BOSTON AMER.
1

BAKER, ATHLETIC, A. L.
2

This Card is one of a New Set of
30 BALL PLAYERS

1. DAVIS, Athletics
2. CONNIE MACK, Athletics
3. THOMAS, Athletics
4. BAKER, Athletics
5. DOOIN, Phila. Natl.
6. McQUILLAN, Phila. Natl.
7. KONETCHY, St. Louis Natl
8. KARGER, St. Louis Natl.
9. MOWRAY, St. Louis Natl.
10. MURRAY, St. Louis Natl.
11. LAJOIE, Cleveland
12. ROSSMAN, Cleveland
13. RUCKER, Brooklyn
14. JENNINGS, Detroit
15. DONOVAN, Detroit
16. DELAHANTY, Detroit
17. MULLIN, Detroit
18. ARRELANES, Boston Am.
19. SPENCER, Boston Am.
20. KLING, Chicago
21. PFISTER, Chicago
22. BROWN, Chicago
23. TINKER, Chicago
24. CLARK, Pittsburg
25. GIBSON, Pittsburg
26. ADAMS, Pittsburg
27. AMES, N. Y. Natl.
28. MARQUARD, N. Y. Natl.
29. HERZOG, N. Y. Natl.
30. MYERS, N. Y. Natl.

Previous Series 25, making total issue 55 Cards

PHILADELPHIA CARAMEL CO.
Camden, N. J.

This card is one of a set of the
following 30 BALL PLAYERS

1 "CHRISTY" MATHEWSON, N.Y.N.
2 McGRAW, New York National
3 "JOHNNY" KLING, Chicago Nat.
4 CHANCE, Chicago National
5 "HANS" WAGNER, Pittsburg Nat.
6 CLARKE, Pittsburg National
7 BRESNAHAN, St. Louis National
8 HAL CHASE, New York American
9 FORD, New York American
10 "TY" COBB, Detroit American
11 "HUGHEY" JENNINGS, Det. Am.
12 BENDER, Philadelphia American
13 "ED" WALSH, Chicago American
14 "CY" YOUNG, Cleveland American
15 BRIDWELL, New York National
16 "MINER" BROWN, Chicago Nat.
17 MULLIN, Detroit American
18 "CHIEF" MEYERS, N. Y. National
19 VAUGHN, New York American
20 DOOIN, Philadelphia National
21 TENNY, New York National
22 McLEAN, Cincinnati National
23 LAJOIE, Cleveland American
24 TINKER, Chicago National
25 EVERS, Chicago National
26 DAVIS, Philadelphia American
27 COLLINS, Philadelphia American
28 BILL DAHLEN, Brooklyn Nat.
29 CONNIE MACK, Phila. American
30 COOMBS, Philadelphia American

"MINER" BROWN, CHICAGO NAT'L
3

Wagner, s.s. Pittsburg Nat'l
4

Smith's MELLO-MINT
TRADE MARK
THE TEXAS GUM

This Picture is one of the series of 50 Base-Ball Players, one of which is wrapped with each 5¢ package of SMITH'S MELLO-MINT GUM, manufactured only by THE TEXAS GUM COMPANY, INC., TEMPLE, TEXAS.

N. RUCKER, Brooklyn
The Williams Caramel Co. Oxford, Pa.
5

1   This handsome card of Edward Cicotte, valued at $25, shows the hurler before he fell from grace following the Black Sox scandal. It belongs to a series, simply titled "25 Ball Players," that was issued by Philadelphia Caramel in 1909.

2   Frank "Home Run" Baker is pictured here on a Philly Caramel card ($75) issued in 1910. Baker earned his nickname by leading the American League in round-trippers four straight years, 1911–1914, and by slugging crucial homers off Mathewson and Marquard in the 1911 World Series.

3   Another "anonymous" caramel series, issued in 1911, contains thirty subjects. Illus-

trated: the card of Mordecai Brown ($100), Hall of Fame pitcher, who answered to the nicknames "Three-Finger" and "Miner."

4   "Mello Mint" caramel cards were distributed by the Texas Gum Company and are rarely found outside the Lone Star State. Any card from the set is worth a minimum of $45; a superstar like Honus Wagner sells for $350.

5   George Napoleon Rucker, bellwether of the Brooklyn pitching staff for nearly a decade, appeared in the Williams Caramel series of 1910 ($50). Strangely enough, his card does not list his position, the only card in the set to omit this vital information.

CLARKE
Pittsburg

COBB, DETROIT AMER.

JACKSON CLEVELAND

1   2   3

4

1-3   This clever idea — thin-paper baseball-player discs packed in round tin containers — was the last-gasp effort of a venerable gum company about to vanish from the marketplace forever. A common player of the borderless set (16-1) sells for $15; the scarcer red-border variety (16-3) is worth $35. The square paper card of Clarke at center ($35) is said to be a Colgan "proof," but it is more likely a related set issued by another firm.

4   "Texas Tommy," a sepia-photo series issued in 1914, is rarely found in Texas. The name more likely refers to a candy product marketed in northern California. The best of the known cards in this obscure series is that of Joe Jackson tracking down a fly ball ($750).

Variations on a Theme

Two cards of Ty Cob from the same set! At left, the "regular" card — worth $500 — has the player's name and team at the bottom and the normal checklist of ball players in the series is printed on the back. The card at right is an identical pose but has the name and team printed in white script at the top of the picture. It was cut by hand from a cardboard advertising sheet promoting the confections of the Philadelphia Caramel Company. Both cards were printed in 1909, but the advertising card is the scarcer of the two and carries a price tag of $600.

1 CENTER FIELD
Birmingham, Cleveland Amer.

3 JOSS, CLEVELAND AMER.

5 N.Y. McGRAW

2 PENNANT Chocolates THE BIG HIT "Made by Darby" KID ELBERFELD

4

6 CHICAG WALSH P. CHI. AM.

1 The cards of this scarce candy-box set distributed by Dockman in 1910 have a major flaw — the artwork does not resemble the players. Hence the value: only $10 for a common player like Birmingham.

2 Found nailed to a barn wall! This 1910 Pennant Chocolate card of Kid Elberfeld shows damage but is still marketable at $200. The candy maker, Darby, printed a card on the front and back of every Pennant Chocolates box. Few have survived.

3 An interesting candy-box card from 1910. Sixty subjects, all head photos from certain normal-size caramel cards, are known. Hall of Fame pitcher Addie Joss, appropriately framed in black, is valued at $35.

4 What a deal for a penny! Not only did you get a delicious piece of caramel candy, but a giant die-cut "Action Picture" of a ball player as well! How times have changed: nowadays, any of the cards of this 1910 American Caramel issue will cost you a minimum $500, no candy included.

5 John McGraw, the famous Giants manager, is pictured on this candy-box card issued in 1910 ($50). Advertised as a series of 144, less than thirty subjects have been discovered to date.

6 Neither the date nor company of issue is known for this blank-backed card of White Sox stalwart "Big Ed" Walsh ($50). Most likely it was cut from a candy box marketed during the period 1908–1912.

What a pitching staff these guys would make! Here are eight mound immortals, pictured in a 1908 set published by postcard manufacturer D. E. Rose. They had 2,260 victories against a fearsome array of batters led by the likes of Cobb and Wagner. It's easy to understand why each of these cards sells for $100!

Easily the most popular and desirable of
all the early candy and gum issues, Cracker Jack
cards were released to the public in 1914 and
1915. Many Federal League players are pictured
since the series coincided with the brief two-year
existence of "that other major league." This
gallery of Cracker Jack stars has the following
values: Cobb, $2500; Wagner and Mathewson,
$600 each; Johnson, $750; Lajoie, $350;
Alexander, $300.

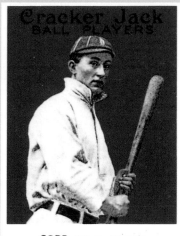

COBB, Detroit - Americans

WAGNER, Pittsburgh - Nationals

MATHEWSON, New York - Nationals

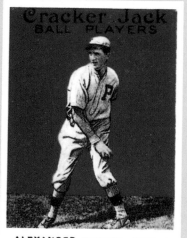

ALEXANDER, Philadelphia - Nationals

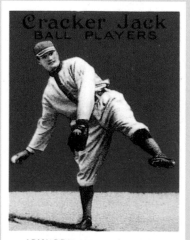

JOHNSON, Washington - Americans

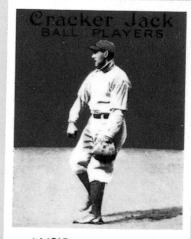

LAJOIE, Philadelphia - Americans

"Where Do Cards Come From?"

1909   1910   1914

1910

Question: how many baseball cards can be made from a single picture? Answer: as many as the public is willing to buy! This picture of Tiger hurler "Wild Bill" Donovan was taken by a baseball photographer named Armiger and it appeared in many early baseball guides. The photo was "adopted" and "enhanced" into a color pose which surfaced in a number of different sets. The cards illustrated were issued by both cigarette and caramel companies; there are only slight variations in background and uniform detail among the four. Many cards in sets produced by various manufacturers were "designed" by enhancing well-known player photographs.

"T-206" is a simple catalog reference number indicating the 206th set in an early list of twentieth-century tobacco issues. It is a humble designation for the most fabulous and popular baseball series ever created. A "monster" set, a collector once declared, and rightly so, not only in length (524 cards), but also in difficulty. Collecting T-206 is the hobby's Mount Everest: many start the climb, but few reach the summit.

1 What accounts for the scarcity of the Eddie Plank card ($9000) in T-206? Color variations suggest a printing problem, but Plank may have also demanded — and not received — compensation from hardnosed James Duke, president of the American Tobacco Company.

2-3 Several players in T-206 appear with misspelled names. Only one card, that of Sherry Magee, was corrected. At left, the "error" card has the name spelled "Magie" ($7000); at right, the corrected version ($35). Beware! The proper spelling is sometimes doctored by scraping away the horizontal lines from the first E but the un-natural spacing that results is a dead giveaway.

4 What a difference a phrase makes! This card of Larry Doyle is captioned "Doyle, N.Y." and it sells for $40. The very same card with a caption reading "Doyle, N.Y. Nat'l" — unnoticed by collectors until recently — has sold for $10,000!

Many players changed teams in the three-year span that T-206 was distributed, but only nine team changes are recorded on the cards themselves. Of those nine, the three pictured here are the rarest:

Name	"Before" team & value		"After" team & value	
Demmitt	N.Y. American	$35	St. Louis American	$2250
Elberfeld	N.Y. American	$40	Washington	$750
O'Hara	N.Y. National	$35	St. Louis National	$2250

5-8 The most expensive of the "regular" T-206's are the four cards depicting baseball immortal Tyrus Raymond Cobb. In this case, price variations reflect subtle differences in scarcity and demand: (21-5), $850; (21-6), $1500; (21-7), $900; (21-8), $850.

Piedmont — no change

Sweet Caporal — no change

Sovereign — +10%

Old Mill — +10%

Polar Bear — +10%

Cycle — +15%

Tolstoi — +15%

El Principe de Gales — +15%

American Beauty — +15%

Hindu (brown) — brown +15%

Hindu (red) — red +35%

Broad Leaf — +40%

Carolina Brights — +40%

Lenox — +50%

Uzit — +60%

Drum — +100%

"Take a Look Back . . . Literally!"

The cards of T-206 were distributed in packages of sixteen different cigarette brands manufactured by the American Tobacco conglomerate. Some of these brands were nationally known; others were exclusively regional. The result is a pecking order of scarcity among the brands that may increase the value of any card. The effect, if any, of the brand advertising on card values is noted under each illustration.

Does it exist? Burdick's 1938 and 1946 catalogs listed Hustler as one of the T-206 brands, but no cards with Hustler backs have been confirmed. Such a card would be worth a minimum of $5000.

Backs with advertising that reads "Ty Cobb, King of the Tobacco Smoking World" to date have been found only with the red-background portrait of Ty Cobb on the front of the card. Fewer than ten specimens have been reported, and each carries a minimum market value of $6000.

From time to time, a collectible transcends the boundaries of its particular hobby and becomes a legend among the population in general. In stamps, it was the British Guiana 1856 1¢; in coins, the 1913 Liberty nickel. In the realm of baseball cards, it is the American Tobacco Company's 1909 baseball card of Honus Wagner.

Veteran card collectors as well as neophytes attending their first

1

convention, housewives and investment bankers who read about it in the newspapers or see it on TV—they all refer to it as "the Wagner." The term has even become a part of our vernacular: "You're holding that like it's a Wagner!" How valuable is this card? The price-guide listing of $90,000 is perhaps more plausible than possible; with one exception, actual sales prices have been much lower.

Fact And Fiction About "The Wagner"

2   Fact: Unbelievable, but true! The card you see here is not genuine: it is a watercolor produced in 1937 for a special reason. When the first Wagner was discovered, many hobbyists doubted its authenticity. The owner responded to several requests for proof by sending the actual card through the mail! Upon reflection, he decided it would be better to send a copy, so he painted one. The card that served as his model — the very first Wagner known to collectors — is now part of the Burdick Collection in New York's Metropolitan Museum of Art.

3/4   Fact: There are two players named Wagner in T-206. The card of Pittsburgh's Honus (23-1) is the most valuable trading card of all. The other Wagner, also a shortstop, appears in a Boston American League uniform on these two cards. Nicknamed "Heinie" by his peers, he is better known as "Foolsgold" among card collectors because of the many times he's been mistaken for the genuine rarity.

Fiction: The rarest card? Not by a long shot. In quantitative terms, there are many scarcer cards, but none has the charisma of the Wagner. He was the most popular baseball star pictured in the most popular baseball set ever issued, and his card disappeared mysteriously from circulation almost immediately after it was issued. That's how legends are born. Luckily, the card has reappeared in sufficient numbers to guarantee availability and demand; if it were unique, it would qualify only as a priceless museum piece.

Fact: You can find one! Despite its fabulous reputation and hefty price tag, several Wagners have been found by collectors in recent times. One was even discovered in a stack of nonsports tobacco cards! Reduce the odds: tell everyone you collect tobacco cards and visit all the flea markets, antique dealers, and garage sales you can find. Persistence can be as important as sheer luck.

2   3   4

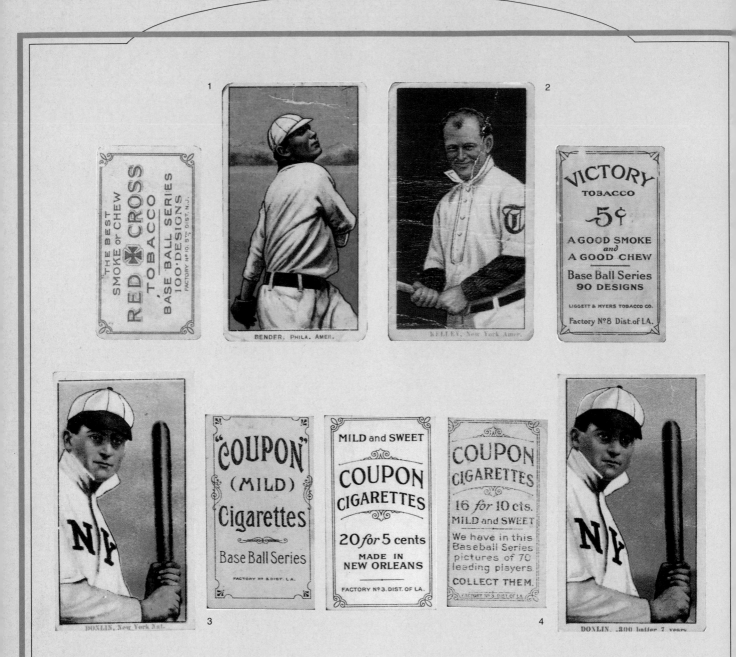

¹ The baseball cards of T-206 were so popular that they were used in other sets until 1919. This Red Cross tobacco card of Bender, issued in 1911-1912, is far scarcer than its counterpart in T-206. It is worth less to collectors, however, because it is a repeat design in a less popular set ($75).

² The very rare Victory Tobacco brand advertising on the back of this Joe Kelley card makes it more valuable ($200) than the same card in T-206 ($150).

³/⁴ "Coupon" cigarettes, a Louisiana brand, incorporated the pictures of T-206 in three separate series over a nine year span. Only the captions were changed to reflect changes in team affiliations. Although scarcer, the typical "Coupon" card is usually found creased and always is priced lower than comparable T-206 cards: 1910-11 series . . . $35; 1914-15 series . . . $20, 1919 series . . . $30. The double cards of Donlin — one with a team caption ($20), the other with an unusual "achievement" phrase ($30) — belong to the 1914-15 set.

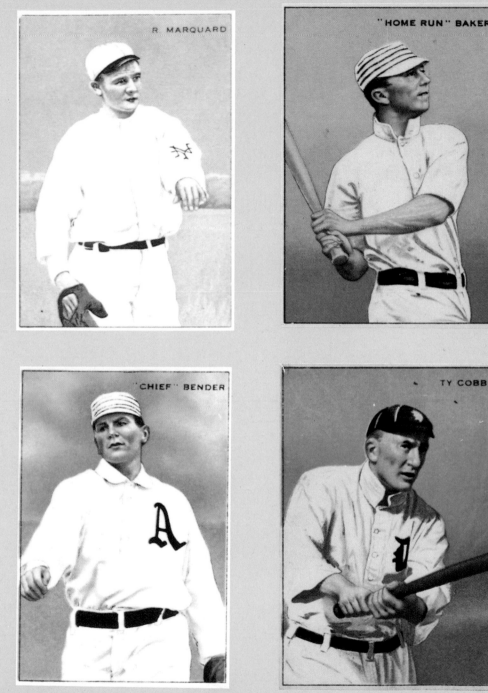

The four baseball players that appeared among the twenty-five cards in 1912 "Series of Champions" were chosen for their outstanding performances the previous season. Marquard ($200), a bonus-baby bust in three earlier tries, blossomed into a 24-game winner. Baker ($200) led the American League in home runs and socked "taters" off Mathewson and Marquard in consecutive World Series games. Bender ($200), a money pitcher if there ever was one, had crucial victories throughout the season and posted two World Series wins. All Cobb ($750) did was hit .420!

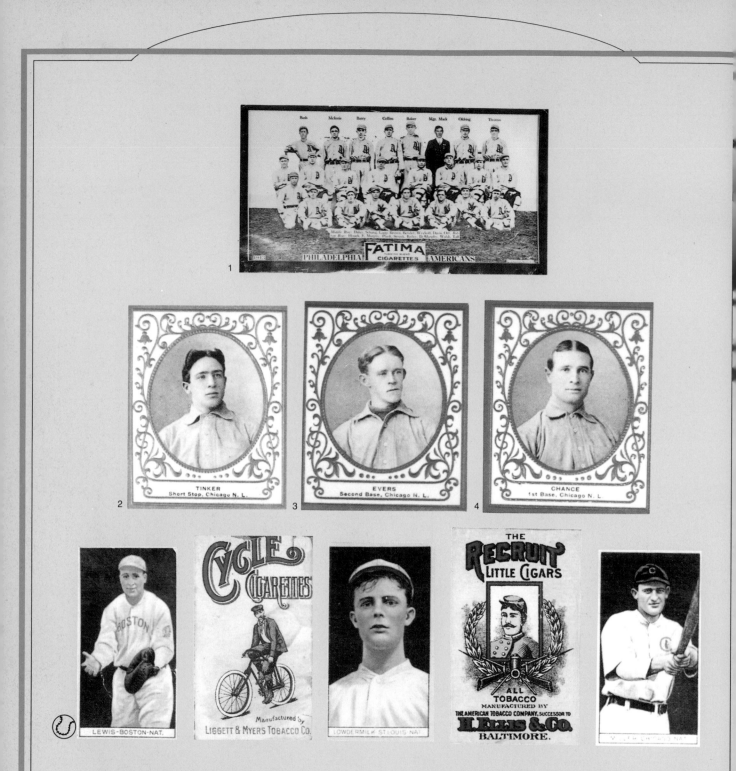

1   There are five future Hall of Fame players pictured on this "Philadelphia Americans" photograph ($125) issued in the Fatima cigarettes team series of 1913: Collins, Baker, Mack, Bender, and Plank.

2-4   *"These are the saddest of possible words, Tinker to Evers to Chance."* They didn't invent the double play, they simply perfected it. Here the rally killers ($150 each) are depicted in ornate portrait cards issued with Ramly and T.T.T. cigarettes in 1909.

This 1912 baseball series doesn't get any respect! It's filled with great players and interesting biographies, but many collectors believe that the monotonous brown background ruins the set. However, those who collect the set respect it for the rare cards it contains: Lewis ($2000), Lowdermilk ($2000), and Miller ($1800)!

The "Base Ball Folder Series" issued with Mecca cigarettes in 1911 employs a clever flip-up design by which two players shared the same pair of legs! Although the tandem of Ty Cobb and Sam Crawford will cost you plenty ($500), the key to completing the set is the scarce card picturing Patsy Dougherty and Harry Lord ($250).

The color-portrait end panels fold over the black-and-white center picture in this remarkable American Tobacco set issued in 1912. The card of Jennings and Cobb ($1200) is the most expensive in the set, but collectors will find it more difficult to obtain the numerically scarcer Birmingham/Turner combination ($250).

1   Baseball "blankets" — actually squares of felt — not only are unique in design, but are also undervalued: a common player may be purchased for as little as $10. Issued in 1914, each blanket was folded into a manila envelope and attached to a pack of Egyptian Straights cigarettes.

2/3   Want to play dominoes with your favorite ballplayer? It was possible to do so with the Sweet Caporal cigarette set of "Domino Discs." The cardboard center containing the picture is the size of a quarter and is protected by a 1/8″ metal rim. Parent ($15) and Reulbach ($20) are two of the 129 discs reported to date.

4/5   Popular hobbies before the Great War of 1914 included scrapbook pictures, postcards, and stamp collecting. The American Tobacco Company tried to tap such interests by issuing a series of baseball and actress stamps with Helmar cigarettes in 1911. Low demand for this scarce set has kept values down: Bush and Mullin sell for $12 each.

6   Louis Evans of the Cardinals is one of a series of baseball-player portraits that were issued in boxes of Turkey Red cigarettes in 1911. Popularly known as "silks," the designs are actually printed on satin and are typically valued at $30 with the cardboard backing intact ($15 without it).

7   Piedmont baseball-player "art stamps," issued with cigarettes of the same name, appeared in 1914-15. They were part of a larger group of designs that included military uniforms, animals, birds, flags, fish and national types. Rarely found in top condition, a player of Wilson's caliber lists for $35.

Even as the final run of cards in the highly successful white-border baseball series (T-206) was being distributed in 1911, the American Tobacco Company launched an exciting and totally new set into the marketplace. Commonly called "Gold Borders," it appears that these cards specifically targeted major-league cities in the East and Midwest. Every card in the set, except the twelve minor leaguers, is a portrait: National League players have solid backgrounds; American League players have baseball diamond backdrops. Cobb ($1350), Johnson ($650), Joss ($350), Mathewson ($400), Speaker ($300), and Young ($350) lead the value parade, but the scarce cards of Graham and Shean ($350 each) are the toughest "outs" in the set.

Variations on a Theme

Variety adds spice and value! The closed-mouth portrait of Bresnahan sells for $150, but with mouth open he sells for $300. The same is true for Collins. Bobby Wallace is doing a hat trick: he's worth more without his cap ($300) than with it ($150). Finally, a case where less is more: it seems that George Wiltse is more valuable with only one ear ($175) than he is with two ($50).

Big prices for big cards! Extra-large-size premium issues, or "cabinet cards," were as popular in the early twentieth century as they had been in the 1880s and 1890s. Illustrated: Fred Luderus, in a series of Plow Boy Tobacco Cubs and White Sox issued in 1910 ($100); "Bugs" Raymond, in the Turkey Red set ($200), the finest cabinet cards ever printed; Sporting Life cabinet of Chase ($300) is similar in design to Turkey Red cards; John Morrisey, from the burgundy-tint, faux gravure series published by Sporting Life ($100).

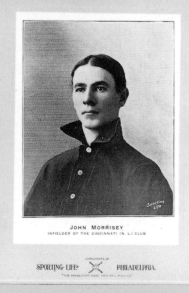

Bakery Cards Can Cost
A Lot of Bread

1-5   The gorgeous color artwork of this 1911 set makes it a favorite among collectors. Issued concurrently by several different bakery chains, twelve of the twenty-five cards in the set picture Hall of Fame baseball players. Values for the players illustrated: Bender ($75), Merkle ($35), Young ($100), Wagner ($250), and Cobb ($400).

6   The Philadelphia Athletics, world champions of 1910, were honored in this Rochester Baking series issued the following year. Except for the advertising on the back, the eighteen cards in the set are identical to the Fireside cigarette series. Manager Connie Mack was forty-eight years old and had been in professional baseball for twenty-four years when this card, now worth $300, was printed.

"Oliver Kirby 'Redbuck' White,
Threw the ball with all his might."

7   After posting a 7-15 slate with Boston, Oliver "Redbuck" White was traded to Pittsburgh shortly after the start of the 1910 season. He arrived in time to be included in Tip Top Bread's card series honoring the 1909 world champion Pirates team — a team he was not on! Andy Warhol was right: everyone becomes famous, at least momentarily! Value of card: $75.

8   Hal Chase, one of the slickest first-sackers to play the game, joined the Reds in 1916 after playing in the Federal League for a season and a half. This red-background portrait of "Prince Hal," a picture that appeared in several earlier candy sets, has advertising for the General Baking Company printed on the back ($25).

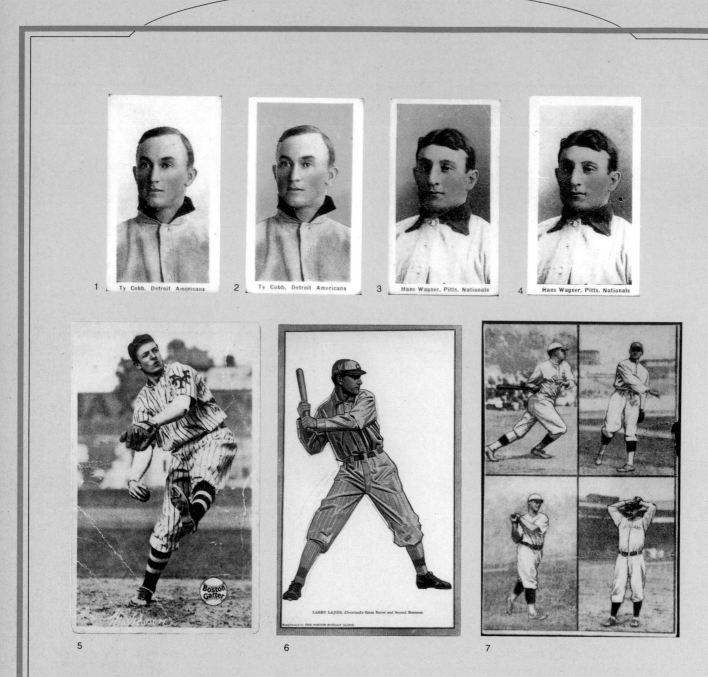

1 Ty Cobb, Detroit Americans 2 Ty Cobb, Detroit Americans 3 Hans Wagner, Pitts. Nationals 4 Hans Wagner, Pitts. Nationals

5

6 LARRY LAJOIE, Cleveland's Great Batter and Second Baseman
Supplement to THE BOSTON SUNDAY GLOBE

7

1-4 Shades of blue make a big difference in the Sporting Life newspaper series of 1911. Light-blue backgrounds on Cobb ($900) and Wagner ($300) are considered normal; scarce dark-blue backdrop automatically doubles the value of these cards.

5 Boston Garter baseball pictures were given to clothing merchants to induce them to carry this line of apparel. The cards were often used as window advertising, and customers frequently asked for them. The green-tone card of Mathewson is not handsome, but it is valuable ($250).

6 As a bonus to purchasers, the *Boston Globe* newspaper added baseball-player supplements to its Sunday editions in 1911. This beautifully colored sketch of Larry "The Frenchman" Lajoie ($150) is a premium rarely seen by collectors.

7 No other copy of this rare baseball four-in-one card has ever been seen! It dates from 1919 and pictures four Hall of Famers: Babe Ruth (batting, in a Boston uniform), Walter Johnson, Stan Covelski, and George Sisler. Valued at $1000, it is printed on thick cardboard and is devoid of any identifying marks.

The Fabulous Twenties

CARL MAYS
PITCHER, NEW YORK AMERICANS

RAY CHAPMAN
S. S.—Cleveland Americans
30

A decade of social and economic upheaval in America, the 1920s are known to card collectors as a wasteland. Both the quality and quantity of baseball cards took a quantum leap backward from the idyllic period of 1909-1912.

And why not? James Duke, the architect of that trading-card renaissance, and his American Tobacco Company had been virtually expelled from the domestic market by antitrust legislation. The herd of locally based companies that followed abandoned "advertising inserts" — trading cards — for other forms of promotion.

When the cigarette companies stopped producing trading cards, only candy and gum manufacturers remained. Throughout the 1920s and the Great Depression, the low retail cost of gum and confections, usually 1¢ per piece, made such items popular and affordable. It also limited the amount of revenue available for planning and printing trading cards. Only in the 1930s, when the bubble-gum fad really took off, did volume sales enable companies to spend more

time and money on trading-card production.

A particularly dull-witted explanation for the dreary baseball cards of the 1920s pins the blame on the Black Sox scandal and the pall of gloom it cast over the American public. That gloom, if it ever existed, disappeared with the thunderous crack of Babe Ruth's bat and the wonderful caliber of play of the "live ball" era. Baseball was never more popular than it was in the 1920s; the baseball-card drought of the period was simply the result of non-baseball economic factors.

Major-league baseball began the decade of the Twenties on a dreadful note when Ray Chapman, shortstop of the pennant-winning Cleveland Indians, was beaned by a rising fastball thrown by Yankee submariner Carl Mays. Chapman died in a New York hospital on August 17. Rookie Joe Sewell, a future Hall of Famer, played shortstop for the Indians the final twenty-two games of the season.

1 EDDIE CICOTTE 2 KID GLEASON 3 EDDIE COLLINS

4 RUBE MARQUARD 5 FRANK FRISCH 6 BABE RUTH

7 BATTER SHORTSTOP CENTER FIELD BATTER SHORTSTOP

1-3 Three of the principals in the Black Sox drama were pictured in an anonymous strip-card set issued in 1920. Left: Cicotte, a star pitcher accused of throwing games ($7); center: Gleason, the honest manager ($7); right: Collins, who claimed he never knew about the fix ($12).

4-6 The same 1920 set also contained cards of these Hall of Fame players from New York's three major-league teams. Rube Marquard ($10) was in his last season in Brooklyn; Frankie Frisch ($12) became the Giants regular third baseman that year; and Babe Ruth ($75), in a Yankee uniform for the first time, belted a record 54 home runs!

7 The most common types of 1920s cards were printed and issued in strips; hence the name "strip card." The length of the strip, generally five or ten cards, depended on the brand and amount of candy that was purchased. Prices for strip cards are generally low, not only because of poor workmanship, but also because most lack manufacturer's identification. This strip of five generic "position" cards ($10) was probably issued about 1920.

1 FRANK BAKER 3RD BASE NEW YORK "YANKEES" A. L. — BERT GALLIA PITCHER ST. LOUIS "BROWNS" A. L. — MILTON WATSON INFIELDER ST. LOUIS "CARDINALS" N. L.

2 WALTER JOHNSON PITCHER WASH'TON "SENATORS" A. L.

Safe at the Home Plate
For Sale at All Grocers
Mother's Bread and Besta Cake
John M. Streett

3 PING BODIE YANKS OUTFIELD — PING BODIE YANKS OUTFIELD

4 ROGER HORNSBY ST. LOUIS SHORT STOP — ROGER HORNSBY ST. LOUIS SHORT STOP

5 BABE RUTH

6 "BABE" RUTH Outfielder N. Y. Yankees, A. L.

7 "BABE" RUTH Outfielder New York Yankees, A. L.

8 "BABE" RUTH YANKEES, A.L.

1   Frank Baker, who earned the nickname "Home Run" in earlier days, socked ten round-trippers while playing third base for the Yankees in 1919. A Boston Red Sox outfielder named Ruth led the American League that year with 29. This three-card strip of Baker, Gallia, and Watson, from an anonymous 1919 series, is worth $25.

2   Card of Walter Johnson, which appears blank-backed in the same 1919 set, has been discovered with bakery advertising on the back, thereby doubling its value to $30.

3-4   More problems with quality control: the action poses in this 1920 strip set were reversed! The first card of each pair is the original and is easily identified by the "IFC" copyright printed on the picture. The reversed poses are not scarce: a brace of Bodies retails for $10; the Hornsby tandem lists for $20.

5-7   Babe Ruth dominated baseball in the Twenties, and his image also dominated the strip-card sets. Card 35-5 hails from a 1920 series and is an actual photo set on an unflattering background ($75). Cards 35-6 and 35-7 ($50 each) belong to a 1924 set and are good examples of the caricature artwork so unpopular with collectors. The picture of a dissipated Babe, card 35-8, was issued in 1926 ($40).

An uncut sheet of cards is always difficult
to come by and will command a premium
beyond the collective value of the individual
cards. This sheet, from a 1927 baseball-player/
playing-card series, contains seven Hall of
Famers and is worth $200.

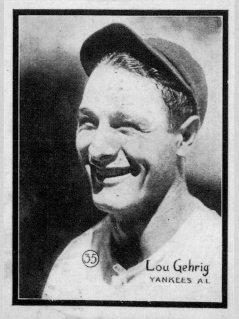

1

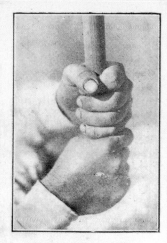

"Babe" Ruth's Grip!

This is how "Babe" Ruth grips his bat as he steps up to add one more home run to his long string. Try it out on your own "Louisville Slugger."

2

Murderer's Row

3   (29) TONY LAZZERI

4   (7) BOB MEUSEL

5   (26) LOU GEHRIG

6   (6) BABE RUTH

1   A portrait of the immortal Lou Gehrig ($500) is the jewel in a 1930 set issued by an unidentified maker. The cards were sold in strips of three for a penny, and a bonus of free candy was given for any strip found with an ink bar printed on the back.

2   A card of a baseball player's batting grip is worth $100! It appeared in a 1928 Fro-Joy ice-cream set of six pictures honoring the mighty Babe Ruth. Fro-Joy cards are scarce because a set could be exchanged for a large "autographed" photo of the Bambino.

3-6   And they really deserved the name! In 1927, the heart of the Yankee lineup terrorized pitchers with these totals: Lazzeri — 18 HR, 102 RBI; Meusel — 8 HR, 103 RBI; Gehrig — 47 HR, 175 RBI; Ruth — 60 HR, 164 RBI. Since the cards of this 1928 series distributed by Tharps and Yeunglings could be turned in for a gallon of ice-cream, collecting Tony ($20), Bob ($20), Lou ($125), and the Babe ($200) can also murder your pocketbook!

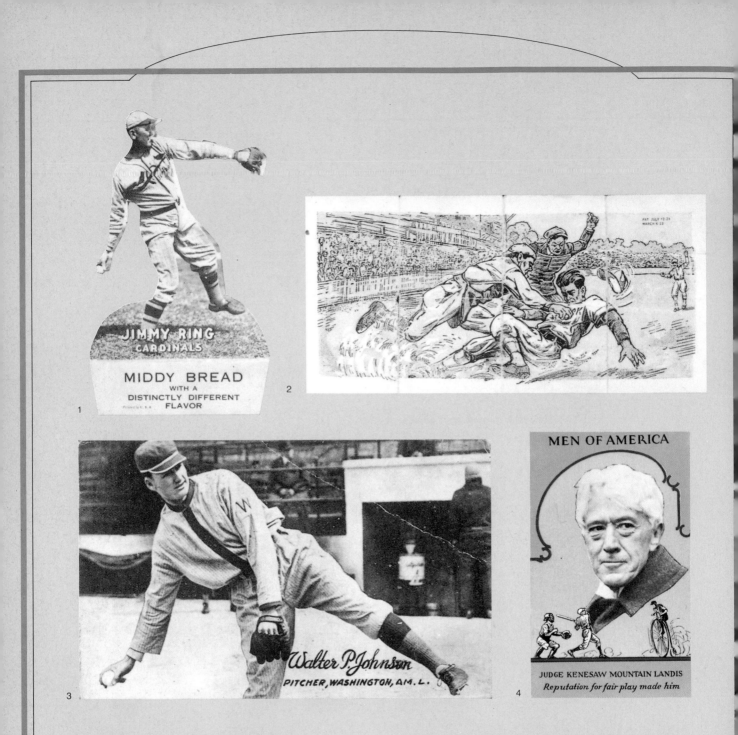

1   JIMMY RING CARDINALS

MIDDY BREAD WITH A DISTINCTLY DIFFERENT FLAVOR

2

3   *Walter P. Johnson* PITCHER, WASHINGTON, AM.L.

4   MEN OF AMERICA

JUDGE KENESAW MOUNTAIN LANDIS
Reputation for fair play made him

1   One of the rarest sets of the Twenties: a series of Cardinals and Browns issued only in the St. Louis area by Middy bread. The die-cut card of Jimmy Ring ($150) dates the set: he pitched for the Redbirds only in 1927.

2   Paint without paint! Color dyes in the paper of this Cracker Jack baseball scene ($25) were released by brushing water on the surface. Issued in the mid-1920s, it has a nifty exposition of the national game printed on the back.

3   The largest cards of the Twenties — called "exhibits" after the company that popularized them — were sold for a penny in arcades and amusement parks. This exhibit card of Walter Johnson, issued in 1921, currently retails for $75.

4   Issued in 1929, this six-page folder ($35) eulogizes Judge Kenesaw Mountain Landis for his sense of fair play. Yet Landis built his career on political leverage and banned amateur ballplayers from signing professional contracts simply because they played alongside barnstorming Black Sox!

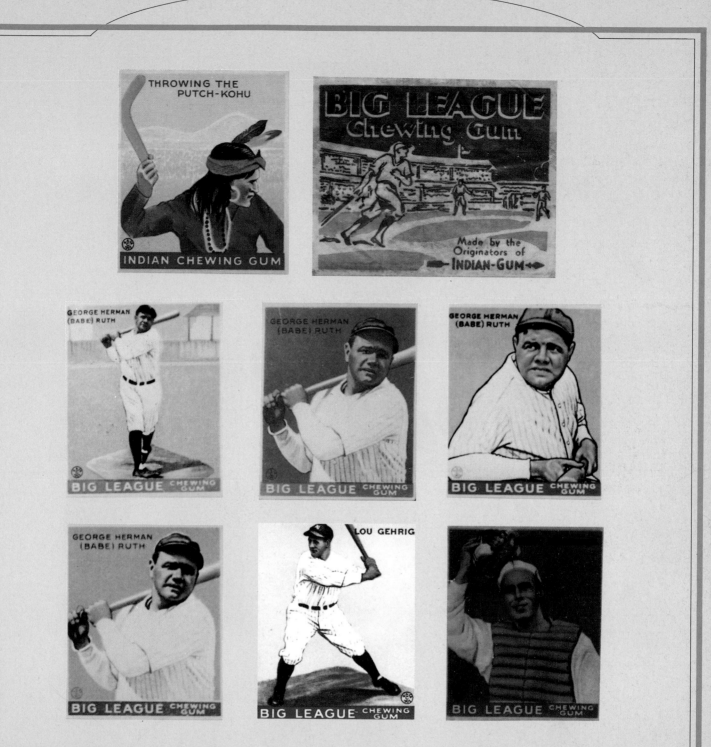

Bubble Gum's Golden Age

It began in early 1933, when "The World's Greatest Penny Value," Goudey's Indian Gum, became a sensational market success. Indian Gum provided the capital needed to produce the 1933 "Big League Ballplayer" series, now considered to be the benchmark baseball set of the prewar bubble-gum era.

The 1933 "Big League" series contains seven bona fide "wallet killers." The batting pose of Ruth, was double-printed and lists for $2400; the three close-ups of the Babe, all single-printed, cost $3000 each. Two cards of Gehrig (nos. 92 and 160) have identical fronts and prices: $1250 each. The initial card of the series, Benny Bengough, is rarely found in excellent condition; it is easily marketable at $1000.

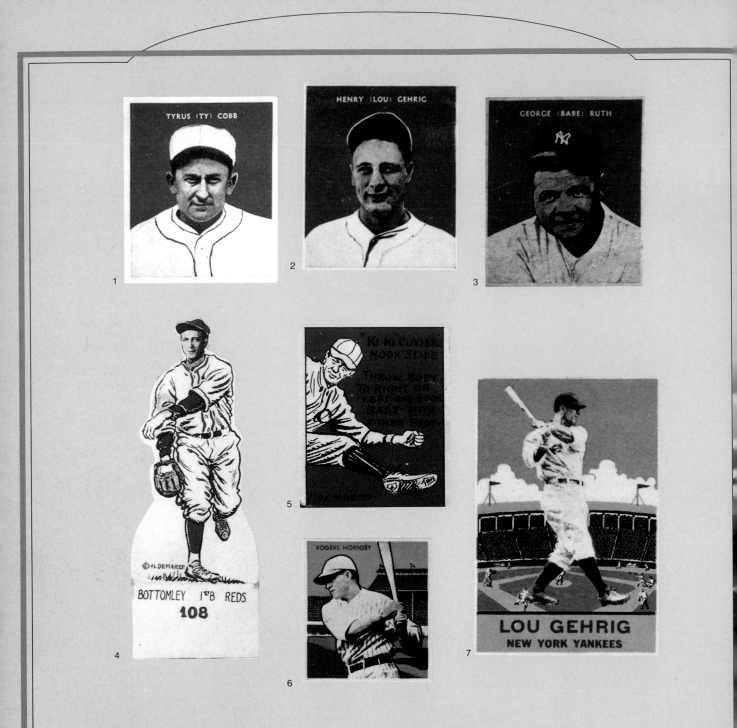

1-3   Portraits of Cobb ($1250), Gehrig ($1350), and Ruth ($1500) highlight the United States Caramel series of 1932. The set is virtually impossible to complete due to a promotional gimmick employed by the company (see page 45).

4/5   Here are two card sets produced by a former ballplayer! Judging from their scarcity, Al Demaree was better at pitching baseballs than baseball cards. The die-cut card of "Sunny Jim" Bottomley ($225) appeared in 1935; "Major League Secrets," containing Ki Ki Cuyler's advice about sliding ($35), was probably issued in 1933.

6/7   The coloration and design of Tatoo-Orbit's 1933 baseball series have restricted its popularity. Hornsby, the key card of this scarce set, lists for only $200. The 1933 Delong card of Lou Gehrig is better designed and is more valuable: $2250.

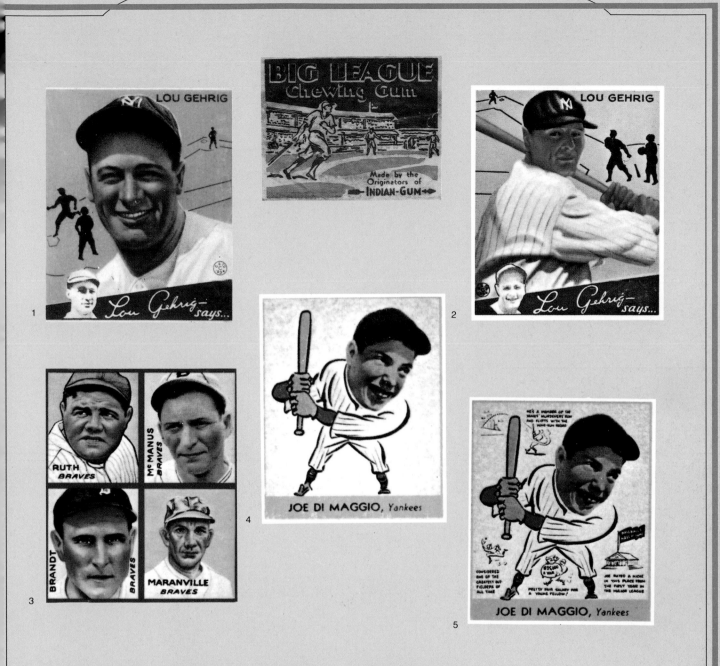

1 LOU GEHRIG

BIG LEAGUE Chewing Gum — Made by the Originators of INDIAN-GUM

2 LOU GEHRIG

3 RUTH BRAVES — McMANUS BRAVES — BRANDT BRAVES — MARANVILLE BRAVES

4 JOE DI MAGGIO, Yankees

5 JOE DI MAGGIO, Yankees

1/2   Goudey returned in 1934 with a special "Lou Gehrig" series of "Big League Baseball Stars." Gehrig's portrait ($1750) and batting ($2000) pictures are the most expensive cards in the set. Babe Ruth, who appeared on four different 1933 Goudeys, did not have a single card in the 1934 set!

3   Cards of the 1935 Goudey series have four player portraits on front and "mystery backs" — sections of nine black-and-white pictures of famous teams and players. This card of Babe Ruth, listing him with the Boston Braves, comes with four different puzzle-section backs, worth a total of $3200.

4/5   Goudey's "Heads Up!" series of 1938 is a favorite among collectors. The twenty-four ball players in the set are all pictured twice on cards with plain and detailed backdrops. This pair of "Joltin' Joe" DiMaggio cards has a current market value of $3900.

1-3 The ball-player pictures in National Chicle's "Batter-Up!" series were die-cut so they could be used as stand-up toys or displays. Issued in 1934–36, most "Batter Ups" can be found in several color tints as well as in black-and-white. Dizzy Dean and Bill Dickey ($250 each) are two of the highest-rated players in the set.

4 Ultrascarce 1933 Butter Cream Confectionery cards were probably issued in candy packages. Many were returned to the manufacturer as entry tickets in a contest. A typical card from the set, like that of Charles Root, sells for $200.

A popular novelty of the 1930s used sunlight to develop images by using contact paper and negatives. M.P. & Co. issued its "Ray-O-Print Outfits" about 1930; this pack included a small metal easel to hold the developed picture of Babe Ruth ($100). The blue-tint "sun picture" of Hall of Fame manager Bill McKechnie ($25) was distributed by Foto-Fun of Cincinnati in 1938.

Here's trouble for collectors of National Chicle's "Diamond Stars" series: the final twelve regularly issued cards of the set. Total value: $3150. Card researchers wonder why these twelve players, all of whom appeared earlier in the series, showed up again at the very end.

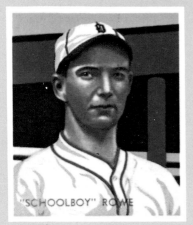

To Sign Or Not To Sign?

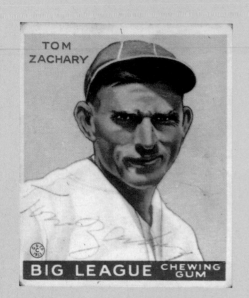

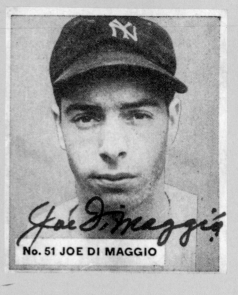

What effect does an autograph have on the value of a card? In terms of resale or investment, a player's signature on a card decreases the value among card collectors, but increases it for autograph buffs. Since there are many more card collectors than autograph hounds, it's best to use photos or other non-card memorabilia for signing. Unmarked cards are *always* easier to sell.

Goudey Gum's 1933–34 series of "Sport Kings" spotlighted the most celebrated athletes of the day. Of the forty-eight cards issued, three represented the national pastime: Cobb ($800), Ruth ($1200), and Hubbell ($175). These cards would be even more valuable today had not cases of "Sport Kings" been dumped on the market in the late 1940s.

The Cards That Never Were

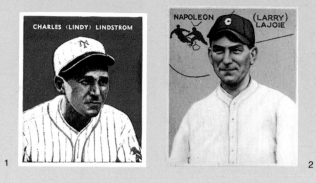

1

2

3

1   A million-dollar card? The owner thinks so, because no other copy has been found since the series was issued in 1932. At that time, the U.S. Caramel Company offered prizes to those completing sets but practically eliminated winners by withholding distribution of Lindstrom, card no. 16. Now that it is known to exist, more copies will undoubtedly be discovered. In the meantime, the card, at least temporarily unique, is snared in a twilight zone of undetermined value.

2   When Goudey Gum printed this card of Napoleon Lajoie in 1934, they were actually responding to complaints about a missing number — 106 — in the 1933 "Big League

Baseball" series. Lajoie cards were sent out directly from the factory when requested and were never distributed in 1934 "Big League" gum packs. This accounts for the scarcity of the card, which currently lists for $10,000.

3   Here is a truly unique group of cards: an uncut printer's-proof sheet from National Chicle's 1936 series "Diamond Stars." For some reason yet unknown, these cards were never put into production and distributed to the public, and their existence remained a secret for more than forty years. Part of a private collection, the sheet would fetch a hefty price if placed upon the market.

AMERICAN LEAGUE PENNANT WINNERS, 1934
Front Row—Lynwood "Schoolboy" Rowe–Herman Clifton–Coach Baker–Joyner White–Mickey Cochrane–Cy Perkins, Coach–Ervin Fox
Second Row–York–Elden Auker–Marvin Owen–Ray Hayworth–Bill Rogell–Vic Sorrell–Tom Bridges–Henry "Hank" Greenberg
Third Row–Hank Schuble–Frank Doljack–Charley Gehringer–Luke Hamlin–Elon Hogsett–Fred Marberry–Goose Goslin
Fourth Row–Trainer Carroll–Bat Boy Willis–Charley Fischer–Alvin Crowder–Gerald Walker

Oversized premium pictures — offered free with purchase or exchanged for wrappers or coupons — were a key area of competition during the "gum wars" of the Thirties. The photo of the 1934 American League Champion Tigers ($20) was issued by National Chicle in 1936. Bob Feller was only twenty-one years of age when his photo ($60) appeared in Goudey's "How To" series of 1939. The exception, not the rule: the only color premiums were marketed by National Chicle during the 1934–36 run of their "Diamond Stars" card series. Great pictures like this photo of Tris Speaker, Ki Ki Cuyler, and Danny Taylor are a bargain today at $20.

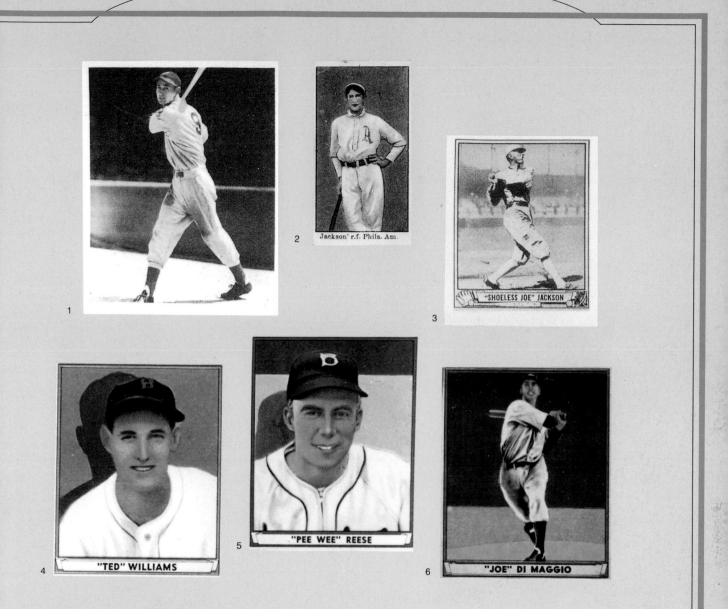

1   2   Jackson' r.f. Phila. Am.   3   "SHOELESS JOE" JACKSON

4   "TED" WILLIAMS   5   "PEE WEE" REESE   6   "JOE" DI MAGGIO

1   In 1939, Gum Inc. — famous for spectacular non-sports sets — used the baseball centennial to launch its premier baseball series: "Play Ball — America." Ted Williams is one of two $1000 cards in this set. (DiMaggio is the other.)

"Say It Ain't So, Joe!"

2/3   This impassioned plea was on the lips of many a baseball fan, young and old, as the newspapers of the day reported the details of the "Black Sox" scandal. "Shoeless Joe" Jackson — as pure a baseball talent as ever graced the diamond — stood accused, with seven other players, of "throwing" the 1919 World Series. All were banned from organized ball for life but many people felt that Jackson had been "railroaded." Fan support for "Shoeless Joe" was still strong twenty years later when his card appeared in the 1940 "Play Ball" baseball series ($700). Also pictured (top): Jackson's "rookie" card, issued in 1909 by the American Caramel Company, now valued at $750.

4-6   Gum Inc.'s 1941 set utilized "colorization" long before Ted Turner ever heard of the word. Many cards in the series were simply colored-in photos from the 1940 set with updated biographies. Williams ($700) and DiMaggio ($1350) are the high-ticket cards in the set, but the picture of young Dodger shortstop Harold "Pee Wee" Reese ($350) is the most appealing.

1 Rabbit Maranville's "How To" instructional folders were given away free to purchasers of "Batter-Up" gum in 1936. Produced by National Chicle, there are twenty folders in the set, each valued at $24.

2 Hall of Famers Carl Hubbell and Mel Ott are part of the 1941 Goudey series, but the card of journeyman pitcher Joe Sullivan ($300) most likely will keep you from completing the set.

3/4 Two types of baseball "movies" issued by Goudey Gum showed action scenes by flipping pages. Top right, Wally Berger of 1938 series ($25); bottom left, Medwick flip book from 1936 ($45) also came with a red cover.

5/6 A picture is worth a thousand words? Baseball strip-cards of the 1930s and 1940s were even worse than their 1920s ancestors. The card of Pete Reiser ($5) was issued in 1943, but the war had nothing to do with its faulty design. A similar pose of Paul Waner belongs to a 1932 set; incredibly, it lists for $60!

War!

With America's entry into World War II, many ball players left their teams to join the armed services. Production of nonessential items like baseball cards stopped immediately as workers and materials were diverted to meet the needs of the war economy. From 1942 to 1946, virtually no trading cards of any sort reached the American public.

BOB FELLER

JOHN WAGNER

LEROY PAIGE

JOE DI MAGGIO

BABE RUTH

Leaf Gum entered the postwar baseball-card market with this multicolor series distributed in 1948–1949. Feller ($1000), Paige ($1650), DiMaggio ($1000), and Ruth ($1200) have impressive price tags, but fifty-seven of the ninety-eight cards in the series list at $100 or more! The card of Honus Wagner dipping chaw ($150) contradicts the popular legend that he despised tobacco.

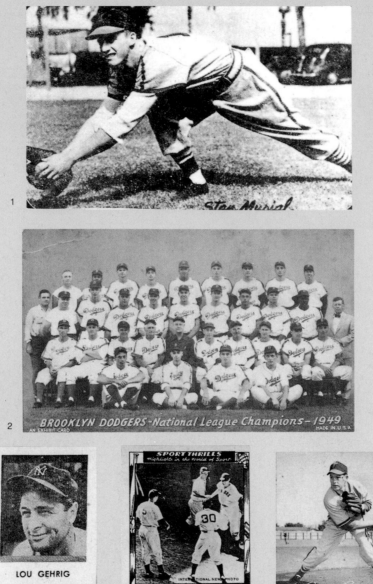

1   Horizontal card of Stan "The Man" Musial ($32) was part of a series given away with Homogenized Bond bread in 1947.

2   How often does the price of a product remain the same for thirty years? Exhibit or arcade cards sold for a penny in 1920, and that's exactly what someone paid for this 1949 Brooklyn team picture (now worth $25) in 1950!

3   This grainy, undistinguished photo of Lou Gehrig ($175) is a key card in the blue-tint strip-card series of 1948–1949.

4   Famous moments in baseball history were forever captured in cardboard by Philly Gum in 1948. Card no. 16, "Williams' Three-Run Homer" (back title), is a key acquisition that lists at $100.

5   Robin Roberts was a twenty-three-year-old pitcher of undetermined worth when this spring-training photo was snapped in 1949. This sticker card of Roberts, issued by two Philadelphia companies, has a very certain value of $100.

LEROY "Satchell" PAIGE

WILLIE MAYS

MICKEY MANTLE

BOSTON
Ted Williams

¹ Yogi Berra looked old at age twenty-three on this 1948 Bowman card ($325).

² On the other hand, forty-three-year-old "Satchell" Paige still looked like a young man when he appeared in the 1949 series ($1000).

³ Classic picture of Jackie Robinson in a batting pose ($450) is one of the many beautiful cards in the 1950 Bowman set.

4/5 Mantle ($5500) and Mays ($1600) were scarce even in 1951 because they appeared in the final run of Bowman cards printed that year.

6/7 A miracle! Baseball cards bearing the Bowman name hit the market in 1989 after an absence of 34 years.

"The Umpire Strikes Back!"

Umpiring is a thankless profession. Every call makes *someone* angry. Close decisions evoke curses and boos. Yet for most arbiters, umpiring is not just a job, but an irresistible calling that requires special skills, judgment, and patience. Often tested by verbal and physical abuse, the umpire seldom retaliates. In 1955, the Bowman Gum Company gave the men in black a measure of revenge by printing thirty-one umpire cards in its baseball series. Total cost: $550. That'll teach you to kick dirt on an umpire's shoes!

Hot Dog!

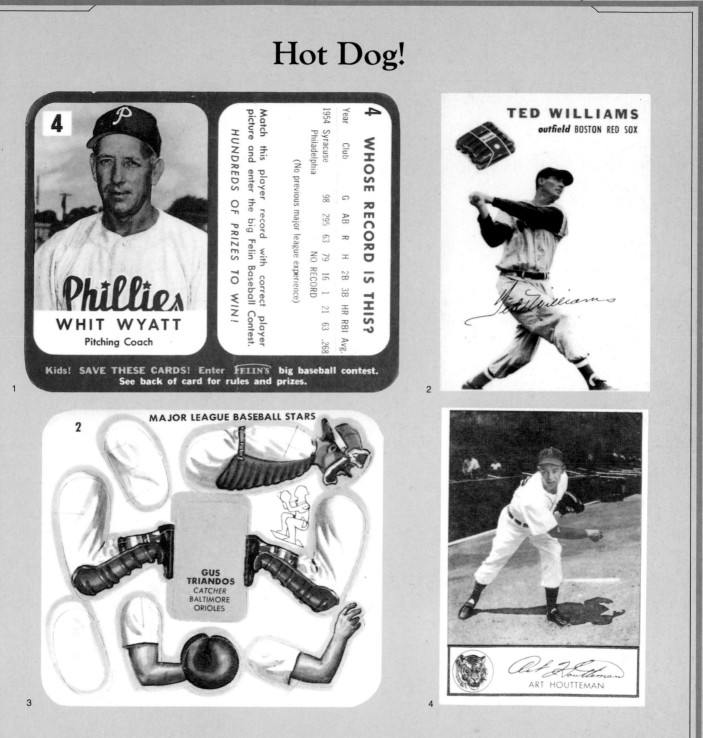

1 America's favorite ballpark food is associated with many card sets. Felin's Franks panel of Whit Wyatt ($100) was heavily waxed to protect the cards while they were in the package.

2 "Ballplayers Maimed By Flying Hot Dogs!" Well, maybe not, but doesn't this 1954 Wilson Wiener card of Ted Williams ($2000) look a bit peculiar to you?

3 Swift produced a set of punch-out-and-assemble ballplayers for distribution in 1957. A typical card from the set, like Gus Triandos, costs $40.

4 One of the nicest hot-dog sets, the 1953 Glendale series of Detroit Tigers, contains a very scarce card of Art Houtteman ($2000).

1/2   The Lefferts Novelty Company of Brooklyn produced Smack-A-Roo candy in 1953. Each diamond-shaped card described a game situation that tested your knowledge of baseball rules. Rarely available, individual cards sell for $35; an intact box is worth $100.

3/4   The baseball theme was also part of the Phoenix "candy & toy" line, which was marketed in the mid-1950s. Each box ($20) contained a novelty item — most often marked "Japan" — like this miniature coloring book ($5).

5-7   "Big League Baseball Lesson" cards ($7 each) were printed on the back panels of Novel Package Corporation candy boxes. Occasionally, the collector will find an intact box ($35), complete with candy and a plastic baseball figure ($10).

8/9   Not many collectors have ever seen one of the "Who Am I?" baseball cards issued by Carnival Candy in 1955. They are ugly, but valuable: current price, $25 each.

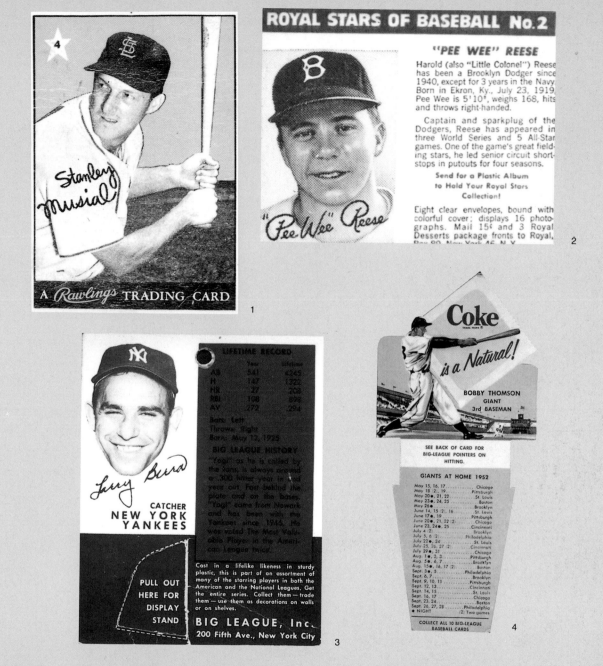

ROYAL STARS OF BASEBALL No.2

"PEE WEE" REESE

Harold (also "Little Colonel") Reese has been a Brooklyn Dodger since 1940, except for 3 years in the Navy. Born in Ekron, Ky., July 23, 1919, Pee Wee is 5'10", weighs 168, hits and throws right-handed.

Captain and sparkplug of the Dodgers, Reese has appeared in three World Series and 5 All-Star games. One of the game's great fielding stars, he led senior circuit short-stops in putouts for four seasons.

Send for a Plastic Album to Hold Your Royal Stars Collection!

Eight clear envelopes, bound with colorful cover; displays 16 photo-graphs. Mail 15¢ and 3 Royal Desserts package fronts to Royal, Box 90, New York 46, N.Y.

"Pee Wee" Reese

LIFETIME RECORD

CATCHER
NEW YORK YANKEES

PULL OUT HERE FOR DISPLAY STAND

BIG LEAGUE, Inc.
200 Fifth Ave., New York City

Coke is a Natural!

BOBBY THOMSON
GIANT
3rd BASEMAN

SEE BACK OF CARD FOR BIG-LEAGUE POINTERS ON HITTING.

GIANTS AT HOME 1952

COLLECT ALL 10 BIG-LEAGUE BASEBALL CARDS

1   Rawlings, the baseball-equipment company, printed trading-cards on the side panels of glove boxes in 1955. All six cards depict Stan Musial. The pose shown here is valued at $150.

2   "Pee Wee" Reese ($60) was one of twenty-four players who appeared on Royal Pudding boxes in 1950. The set must have been popular — it was reissued, with some updates, in 1953.

3   Unusual card of Yogi Berra ($125) was printed on the back of a 1956 package containing a plastic Berra statue. The same group of statues were also given away by Dairy Queen at about the same time.

4   Coca Cola's regional series of carton cards featured players from New York's three major-league teams. Illustrated is the Bobby Thomson card ($150), which is seven inches tall and has batting tips printed on the back.

Marked For Extinction!

"Turkey Red" Cabinets ($35)

1957 Topps ($125)

1956 Topps ($175)

1889 Old Judge Cabinets ($150)

Checklists are the only baseball cards intentionally designed for destruction. Generations of collectors have used pens, pencils, crayons, hole punches, and a variety of other marking devices to draw lines through names or check off boxes. Checklists were folded, flipped, sat on, torn up, or simply thrown away. But no more. Collectors have realized that a clean, unmarked checklist card or cards may be the final, very difficult obstacle to truly completing a set. Here are examples of checklists and checklist values (for unmarked cards only) from four different baseball-card sets.

Fantasy Cards

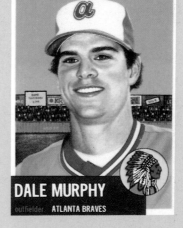

Ted Williams didn't appear in a Topps set until 1954: this 1953 "fantasy card" was created in 1984 for a hobby publication. The Dale Murphy fantasy card, also in 1953 Topps style, is interesting since Murphy wasn't born until 1956!

Baseball For Breakfast

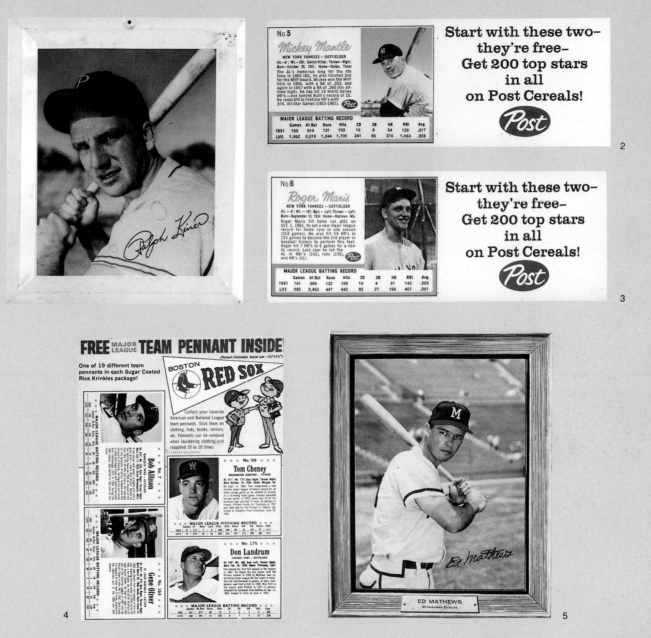

1   There never was a card set quite like this! Metal plaque of Ralph Kiner ($150), with predrilled hole for hanging, came glued to a Wheaties package in 1952. The color picture is printed directly onto the metal surface.

2/3   Unusual Post cereal panel of Bronx Bombers Mickey Mantle and Roger Maris ($100) was an advertising device placed in magazines during the 1962 season.

4   A cereal card on the box is worth two in the hand. "Cut" cards of Allison, Oliver, Cheney, and Landrum cost $1.50, but the intact panel sells for $15.

5   Magnificent color photograph of Eddie Mathews ($200), complete with fake wooden frame and brass name plate, was a Post cereal special edition in 1960.

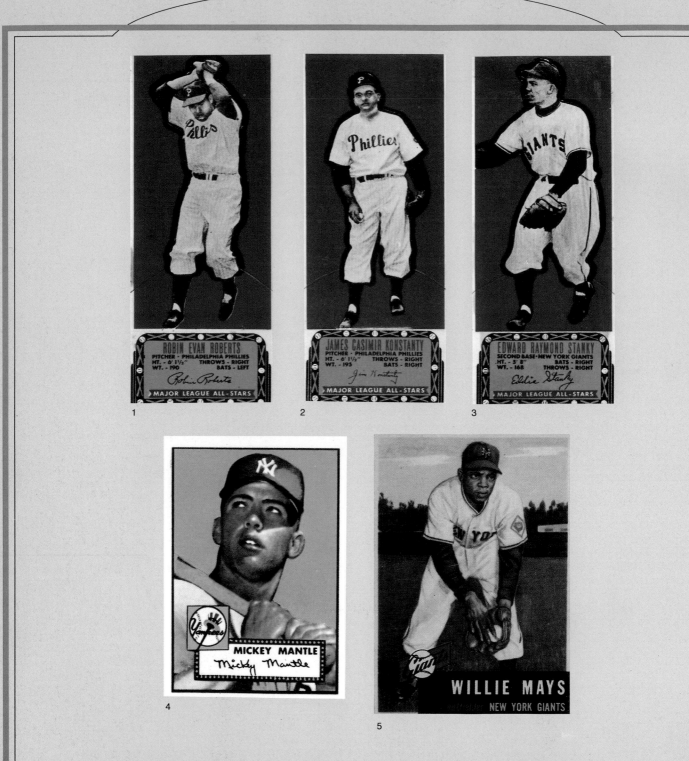

1-3 These three cards from Topps' first baseball set (1951) are worth $25,000! They were never issued in gum packs, like the remaining eight "Current All Stars," but were obtained directly from the company. Roberts lists for $9000, Konstanty and Stanky for $8000 apiece.

4 The first Topps card of Mickey Mantle, issued in 1952, is the most popular card of the postwar era. Although it is not as scarce as many other cards in the set, it is a favorite among collectors and carries a price tag of $6500.

5 Action pose of Giants centerfield sensation Willie Mays is a key card in the 1953 Topps set. It appeared in the scarce "high number" series and is valued at $1400.

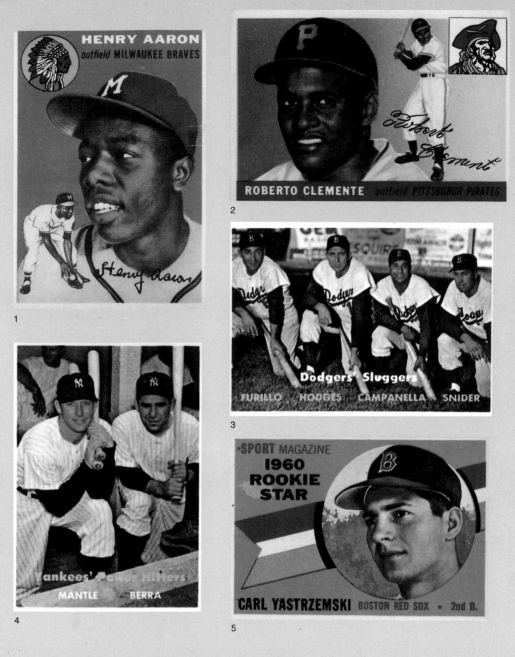

¹ Hank Aaron, the man destined to break the mighty Babe Ruth's career home-run mark, first appeared on a Topps baseball card in 1954 ($800).

² Desire, as well as skill, made Roberto Clemente one of the greatest ball players in baseball history. As a rookie, he broke into the Topps lineup with this 1955 card now valued at $750.

³⁻⁴ Great color photographs make the 1957 Topps set one of the company's best. A modern "Murderer's Row" wearing Brooklyn uniforms appears on the "Dodgers' Sluggers" card ($150). "Yankee Power Hitters" ($250) features Hall of Famers Mickey Mantle and Yogi Berra.

⁵ One of 1989's Hall of Fame inductees, Carl Yastrzemski had humble card beginnings. Undistinguished Topps rookie card of Yaz ($250) appeared in the 1960 set.

Nostalgia Sets, Reprints, And Fakes

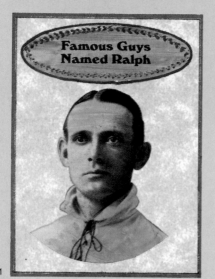

1

MAYO CUT PLUG

REPRINT 1986

2

Jan. 23, 1959 — Ted Signs For 1959

3

Jan. 23, 1959 — Ted Signs For 1959

¹ A "nostalgia" or "collector" set is sold directly to collectors without an accompanying good or service (for example, without gum). Such sets generally carry a low price tag and provide reasonable value in information and pictures. However, if you look at the price guides over a period of years, you will see that such sets rarely increase in value over time. Nostalgia sets should be purchased strictly for fun, not for investment.

² Reprint sets — composed of reproductions of previously issued cards — have increased in popularity as prices for the original cards spiral upward. Most reprint sets are clearly marked, but altered cards and some unmarked reprints from the 1970s continue to surface at flea markets and card shows. If you have doubts about a card, compare it to an original from the same set or seek a second opinion. Reprints are a low-cost alternative to genuine cards, but they will never have resale value beyond the original price.

³ Not all fakes are this easy to spot! The genuine card, on the left, has a tan background, dull white borders, and a "clean" picture area. In contrast, the counterfeit, at right, has a distinct reddish tint, eggshell-white borders, and a cross-hatch pattern running through the picture. The genuine card is worth $225; the fake has no value except as a curiosity.

Baseball At The Movies

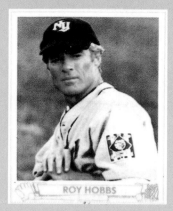

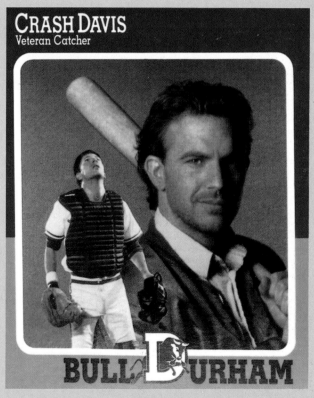

¹ Babe Ruth was pure ham in the 1920s matinee film *The Babe Comes Home*, but the cards commemorating the movie have filet mignon prices: $75 each.

² William Bendix, a former Yankee batboy, portrayed the "Sultan of Swat" in *The Babe Ruth Story*. This 1948 Philly Gum card of Bendix ($10) shows him in a Ruthian pose.

³ Actor Kevin Costner played the role of Crash Davis in the 1988 movie *Bull Durham*. Promotional card ($2) was one of four given away at theaters across the United States.

⁴ This is *not* the card of Roy Hobbs, a.k.a. Robert Redford, that appeared on the screen in *The Natural*. The original card, a mockup of Hobbs in the style of Gum Inc.'s 1940 "Play Ball" series, was not available, so someone created a substitute. It usually sells for $1.

One For The Hall . . .

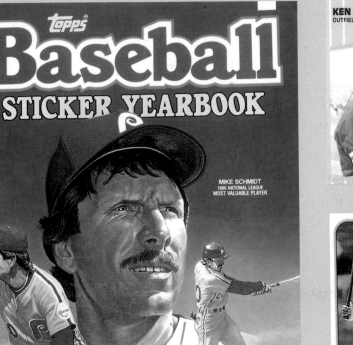

Phillies slugger Mike Schmidt called it quits in 1989 after eighteen years in the "bigs." The best double-threat player to ever man the hot corner, Schmidt always found a way to beat you with his bat or glove. He's a sure bet for Cooperstown, and prices for his cards have already started to move up.

. . . Who Will Follow?

Every spring the guessing game begins anew, for one of baseball's greatest qualities is its unpredictability. Will the Kevin Mitchells and Jose Cansecos of today gain baseball immortality, or will they be forgotten like Mark Fidrych and Joe Charboneau? Only time will tell.

Left table (pages 3–18)

PAGE	CARD	COMPANY	REFERENCE #	YEAR	DIMENSIONS
3	1-2-3	Goodwin	N172	1887-90	1 1/2 × 2 3/4
4	all	Allen & Ginter	N28	1887	1 1/2 × 2 3/4
5	all	Allen & Ginter	N43	1888	2 7/8 × 3 1/4
6	1-2	Anonymous	Y95	1888	2 3/8 high
6	3-4	Buchner	N284	1887	1 3/4 × 3
6	5	Kimball	N184	1888	1 1/2 × 2 5/8
7	all	Goodwin	N162	1888	1 1/2 × 2 9/16
8	1-2	Duke	N142	1893	6 × 9
8	3-4	Newsboy	N566	1894	4 1/4 × 6 1/2
9	center	Goodwin	G58-23-1	1888	7 1/4 high
9	all cards	Goodwin	N173	1888-89	4 1/2 × 6 1/2
10	1	Duke	N154	1888	2 5/16 × 4 1/8
10	2	Young	N360	1892	2 3/16 × 3 7/8
10	3	Duke	N135	1893	2 1/4 × 4 1/8
10	4	Goodwin	N165	1889	1 1/2 × 2 3/4
11	1-2	Breisch-Williams	E107	1903-04	1 3/8 × 2 11/16
12	1-2	American Caramel	E90-1	1909-11	1 1/2 × 2 3/4
12	3	American Caramel	E90-2	1910	1 7/16 × 2 5/8
12	4	American Caramel	E90-3	1910	1 1/2 × 2 3/4
13	1	Dockman	E92	1909-10	1 1/2 × 2 3/4
13	2	Nadja	E92	1909-10	1 1/2 × 2 3/4
13	3-4	Croft & Allen	E92	1909-10	1 1/2 × 2 3/4
13	5	Anonymous	E101	1909-10	1 1/2 × 2 3/4
13	6	Anonymous	E102	1909-10	1 1/2 × 2 3/4
14	1	Standard Caramel	E93	1910	1 1/2 × 2 3/4
14	2	Anonymous	E94	1911	1 1/2 × 2 3/4
14	3	Briggs	E97	1910	1 1/2 × 2 3/4
14	4	Anonymous	None	1910	1 5/16 × 2 1/2
14	5	Anonymous	E97-A	1910	1 1/2 × 2 3/4
15	1	Philadelphia Caramel	E95	1909	1 1/2 × 2 3/4
15	2	Philadelphia Caramel	E96	1910	1 1/2 × 2 3/4
15	3	Anonymous	E98	1911	1 1/2 × 2 3/4
15	4	Texas Gum Co.	E105	1910	1 1/2 × 2 3/4
15	5	Williams	E103	1910	1 1/2 × 2 3/4
16	1	Colgan's	E254	1909-11	1 1/2 dia.
16	2	Anonymous	None	1909-11	1 1/2 × 1 3/4
16	3	Colgan's	E270	1913	1 3/8 dia.
16	4	Texas Tommy	E224	1914	2 5/16 × 3 1/8
16	5-6	Philadelphia Caramel	E95	1909	1 1/2 × 2 3/4
17	1	Dockman	None	1910	1 5/8 × 2 7/16
17	2	Darby	E271	1910	3 1/4 × 4 1/4
17	3	Anonymous	W555	1910	1 3/8 sq.
17	4	American Caramel	E125	1910	7 1/4 high
17	5	Davis	None	1910	1 11/16 × 2 9/16
17	6	Anonymous	None	1909	1 5/8 × 3 1/4
18	all	D.E. Rose	PC760	1909	3 1/2 × 5 1/2

Right table (pages 19–38)

PAGE	CARD	COMPANY	REFERENCE #	YEAR	DIMENSIONS
19	all	Cracker Jack	E145	1914-15	2 1/4 × 3
21	all	American Tobacco	T206	1909-11	1 1/2 × 2 5/8
22	all	American Tobacco	T206	1909-11	1 1/2 × 2 5/8
23	all	American Tobacco	T206	1909-11	1 1/2 × 2 5/8
24	1	Red Cross	T215	1911-12	1 7/16 × 2 5/8
24	2	Victory	T214	1914	1 1/2 × 2 5/8
24	3-4	Coupon	T213	1914-15	1 1/2 × 2 5/8
25	all	American Tobacco	T227	1912	2 5/16 × 3 3/16
26	1	Fatima	T200	1913	2 5/8 × 5 13/16
26	2-3-4	Ramly	T204	1909	2 × 2 1/2
26	baseball	American Tobacco	T207	1912	1 7/16 × 2 5/8
27	top	Mecca	T201	1911	2 1/4 × 4 11/16
27	bottom	Hassan	T202	1912	2 1/4 × 5 1/4
28	1	Egyptian Straights	B18	1914	5 1/4 sq.
28	2-3	Sweet Caporal	PX7	1910	1 11/16 dia.
28	4-5	Helmar	T332	1911	1 1/8 × 1 3/8
28	6	Turkey Red	S72	1911	2 × 3
28	7	Piedmont	T330	1914-15	1 1/2 × 2 5/8
29	all	American Tobacco	T205	1911	1 1/2 × 2 5/8
30	top/left	Plow Boy	T15	1910	5 3/4 × 8
30	top/right	Turkey Red	T3	1911	5 3/4 × 8
30	bottom/left	Sporting Life	M110	1911	5 5/8 × 7 1/2
30	bottom/right	Sporting Life	W600	1909-12	5 1/4 × 7 3/8
31	1-2-3-4-5	Brunners/Weber	D304	1911	1 3/8 × 2 1/2
31	6	Rochester Baking	D359	1911	1 1/2 × 2 5/8
31	7	Tip-Top	D322	1910	1 3/4 × 2 3/8
31	8	General Baking	D303	1916	1 1/2 × 2 3/4
32	1-2-3-4	Sporting Life	M116	1911	1 1/2 × 2 5/8
32	5	Boston Garter	H813	1914	1 9/16 × 2 5/8
32	6	Boston Globe	M140	1910	3 7/8 × 6 5/16
32	7	Anonymous	none	1919	6 × 10
33	left	Neilson's	V61	1921	2 5/8 × 4
33	right	Sporting News	M101-4	1916	2 × 3 1/2
34	1-2-3-4-5-6	Anonymous	W519	1920	1 5/8 × 3
34	7	Anonymous	W552	1924	1 7/16 × 2 7/16
35	1	Anonymous	W514	1919	2 9/16 × 7 3/8
35	2	Streett	D384	1919	2 1/2 × 4 1/2
35	3-4	Anonymous	W516-1	1920	1 7/16 × 2 1/2
35	5	Anonymous	W520	1920	1 7/16 × 2 1/2
35	6-7	Anonymous	W515	1920	1 7/16 × 2 3/4
35	8	Anonymous	W512	1924	1 3/8 × 2 1/4
36	all	Anonymous	W560	1926	1 7/16 × 2 1/4
37	1	Anonymous	W517	1927	7 × 11
37	2	Fro-Joy	F52	1930	3 × 4
37	3-4-5-6	Tharps/Yuengling	F50	1928	2 1/8 × 4
38	1	Middy Bread	none	1927	1 3/8 × 2 1/2
					4 high

PAGE	CARD	COMPANY	REFERENCE #	YEAR	DIMENSIONS
38	2	Cracker Jack	none	1925	$2\frac{1}{2} \times 5$
38	3	Exhibit Supply	W461	1921-24	$3\frac{3}{8} \times 5\frac{3}{8}$
38	4	Stevens-Davis	H572	1929	$2\frac{1}{2} \times 4\frac{1}{8}$
39	all baseball	Goudey	R319	1933	$2\frac{3}{8} \times 2\frac{7}{8}$
40	1-2-3	U.S. Caramel	R328	1932	$2\frac{3}{8} \times 2\frac{7}{8}$
40	4	Al Demaree	R304	1935	$4\frac{3}{8}$ high
40	5	Schutter-Johnson	R332	1933	$2\frac{1}{4} \times 2\frac{7}{8}$
40	6	Tatoo-Orbit	R305	1933	$2 \times 2\frac{1}{4}$
40	7	Delong	R333	1933	2×3
41	1-2	Goudey	R320	1934	$2\frac{3}{8} \times 2\frac{7}{8}$
41	3	Goudey	R321	1935	$2\frac{3}{8} \times 2\frac{7}{8}$
41	4-5	Goudey	R323	1938	$2\frac{3}{8} \times 2\frac{7}{8}$
42	1-2-3	National Chicle	R318	1934-36	$2\frac{5}{16} \times 3\frac{1}{4}$
42	4	Butter Cream	R306	1933	$1\frac{1}{4} \times 3\frac{1}{2}$
42	bottom/left	M.P. & Co.	none	1930	$1\frac{5}{8} \times 2$
42	bottom/right	Foto-Fun	W626	1938	$2\frac{3}{4} \times 3\frac{5}{8}$
43	all	National Chicle	R327	1934-36	$2\frac{3}{8} \times 2\frac{7}{8}$
44	top/left	Goudey	R319	1933	$2\frac{3}{8} \times 2\frac{7}{8}$
44	top/center	American Tobacco	T206	1909-11	$1\frac{1}{2} \times 2\frac{5}{8}$
44	top/right	Gum Inc.	R334	1939	$2\frac{1}{2} \times 3\frac{1}{8}$
44	bottom	Goudey	R338	1933-34	$2\frac{3}{8} \times 2\frac{7}{8}$
45	1	U.S. Caramel	R328	1932	$2\frac{3}{8} \times 2\frac{7}{8}$
45	2	Goudey	R319	1934	$2\frac{3}{8} \times 2\frac{7}{8}$
45	3	National Chicle	R318	1936	$9\frac{1}{4} \times 10\frac{1}{4}$
46	top/left	Goudey	R303-B	1939	$4\frac{3}{4} \times 7\frac{5}{16}$
46	top/right	National Chicle	R312	1936	$4\frac{1}{16} \times 5\frac{3}{8}$
46	bottom	National Chicle	R311	1936	6×8
47	1	Gum Inc.	R334	1939	$2\frac{1}{2} \times 3\frac{1}{8}$
47	2	American Caramel	E90-1	1909-11	$1\frac{1}{2} \times 2\frac{3}{4}$
47	3	Gum Inc.	R335	1940	$2\frac{1}{2} \times 3\frac{1}{8}$
47	4-5-6	Gum Inc.	R336	1941	$2\frac{1}{2} \times 3\frac{1}{8}$
48	1	National Chicle	R344	1936	$3\frac{1}{4} \times 3\frac{5}{8}$
48	2	Goudey	R324	1941	$2\frac{5}{16} \times 2\frac{7}{8}$
48	3	Goudey	R326	1938	2×3
48	4	Goudey	R342	1936	2×3
48	5	M.P. & Co.	R302	1943	$2\frac{1}{4} \times 2\frac{11}{16}$
48	6	Anonymous	R337	1932	$2\frac{5}{16} \times 2\frac{13}{16}$
49	all baseball	Leaf	R401	1948-49	$2\frac{3}{8} \times 2\frac{7}{8}$
50	1	Homogenized Bond	D305	1947	$2\frac{1}{4} \times 3\frac{1}{2}$
50	2	Exhibit Supply	W461	1950	$3\frac{5}{16} \times 5\frac{5}{16}$
50	3	Anonymous	R346	1948-49	$2 \times 2\frac{5}{8}$
50	4	Philadelphia Gum	R448	1948	$2\frac{1}{2} \times 3$
50	5	Lummis/Sealtest	F343	1949	$3\frac{1}{4} \times 4\frac{3}{16}$
51	1	Bowman	R406-48	1948	$2\frac{1}{16} \times 2\frac{1}{2}$
51	2	Bowman	R406-49	1949	$2\frac{1}{16} \times 2\frac{1}{2}$
51	3	Bowman	R406-50	1950	$2\frac{1}{16} \times 2\frac{1}{2}$
51	4-5	Bowman	R406-51	1951	$2\frac{1}{16} \times 3\frac{1}{8}$
51	6-7	Bowman (Topps)	R406-89	1989	$2\frac{1}{2} \times 3\frac{3}{4}$
52	all	Bowman	R406-55	1955	$2\frac{1}{2} \times 3\frac{3}{4}$
53	1	Felin's	none	1955	$3\frac{5}{8} \times 4\frac{1}{2}$
53	2	Wilson	F158	1954	$2\frac{5}{8} \times 3\frac{3}{4}$
53	3	Swift's	F162	1957	$3\frac{1}{2} \times 4$
53	4	Glendale	F151	1953	$2\frac{5}{8} \times 3\frac{3}{4}$
54	1-2	Leffert's	R447	1953	$5\frac{1}{2}$ high
54	3	Phoenix	none	1955	$2\frac{1}{2} \times 3\frac{3}{4}$
54	4	Phoenix	none	1955	$1\frac{11}{16} \times 2\frac{1}{8}$
54	5 & 7	Novel	R322-15	1954	$2\frac{1}{2} \times 3\frac{3}{4}$
54	6	Novel	none	1954	$3\frac{1}{2}$ long
54	8-9	Carnival	R452	1955	$1\frac{7}{8} \times 2\frac{1}{2}$
55	1	Rawlings	UM9	1955	$2\frac{1}{2} \times 3\frac{5}{8}$
55	2	Royal	F219-1	1950	$2\frac{9}{16} \times 3\frac{3}{16}$
55	3	Big League	UM8	1956	4×5
55	4	Coca Cola	F213-9	1952	$7\frac{1}{8}$ high
56	no number	Fez	T3	1910-11	$2\frac{1}{4} \times 2\frac{1}{2}$
56	no number	Topps	R414-57	1957	$2\frac{1}{2} \times 3\frac{1}{2}$
56	no number	Topps	R414-56	1956	$2\frac{5}{8} \times 3\frac{3}{4}$
56	no number	Goodwin	N173	1889	$2\frac{13}{16} \times 5\frac{3}{8}$
56	bottom	B.B.C.	none	1984	$2\frac{5}{8} \times 3\frac{3}{4}$
57	1	Wheaties	PX105	1952	$4\frac{3}{4} \times 5\frac{3}{4}$
57	2	Post Cereal	none	1962	$2\frac{3}{4} \times 7$
57	3	Post Cereal	none	1963	$6\frac{1}{2} \times 8\frac{3}{4}$
57	4	Post Cereal	none	1960	$7 \times 8\frac{3}{4}$
58	1-2-3	Topps	R414-51D	1951	$2\frac{1}{16} \times 5\frac{1}{4}$
58	4	Topps	R414-52	1952	$2\frac{5}{8} \times 3\frac{3}{4}$
58	5	Topps	R414-53	1953	$2\frac{5}{8} \times 3\frac{3}{4}$
59	1	Topps	R414-54	1954	$2\frac{5}{8} \times 3\frac{3}{4}$
59	2	Topps	R414-55	1955	$2\frac{5}{8} \times 3\frac{3}{4}$
59	3-4	Topps	R414-57	1957	$2\frac{1}{2} \times 3\frac{1}{2}$
59	5	Topps	R414-60	1960	$2\frac{1}{2} \times 3\frac{1}{2}$
59	6	Topps	R414-68	1968	$2\frac{1}{2} \times 3\frac{1}{2}$
60	1	MBKA	none	1989	$2 \times 2\frac{3}{4}$
60	2	Anonymous	none	?	$1\frac{1}{2} \times 2\frac{3}{4}$
60	3	Fleer	R418-59	1959	$2\frac{1}{2} \times 3\frac{1}{2}$
61	1	Anonymous	R94	1928	$2\frac{3}{8} \times 2\frac{7}{8}$
61	2	Philadelphia Gum	R421	1948	$2 \times 2\frac{7}{16}$
61	3	Orion	none	1988	4×5
61	4	Anonymous	none	1984	$2\frac{1}{2} \times 3\frac{1}{8}$
62	all cards	Donruss/Fleer/Topps	none	various	$2\frac{1}{2} \times 3\frac{1}{2}$
62	yearbook	Topps	none	1987	$9 \times 10\frac{5}{8}$